MW00616056

"When Will This Pain Ever End?"

A Guide to Finding Your Way Out of the Depths of Despair After

Suffering Profound Grief and Loss

Paula Shaw CADC, DCEP

PAULA SHAW

Paula Shaw Counseling Services

561 Saxony Place, Ste. 101

Encinitas, California 92024

Telephone: (858) 480-9234

Email: PaulaShawCounseling@gmail.com

www.paulashaw.com

The author of this book, Paula Shaw, has provided information and techniques to help you achieve clearing and balancing of the energy system. She is dispensing neither medical nor psychological advice. The author and publisher take no responsibility for the manner in which this information is utilized, nor do they assume liability for any actions or for the results of those actions, which you may take as a result of the information herein contained.

Printed in the U.S.A.

ISBN: 978-0-9963174-1-2

First Edition Printing 2015

Dedication

This book is dedicated to all of you who have trusted me with your pain over the years. You have been beautiful teachers and I hope that I can bring what I learned from you to all those who seek help and healing from this book.

To my daughter, Erin, a beautiful writer herself, who encouraged me to get it done and who rolled up her sleeves and assisted in the production of this book.

To my son Casey, always a fan and a source of support.

To my amazing family, who are my greatest cheerleaders.

To the most incredible friends anyone ever had, the women who sustain me, and the men who make life interesting.

And finally, to the Divine Sources that inspire me, guide me and work with me. My Appreciation and Gratitude in every moment.

Acknowledgements

The writing of this book has been a process that I will never forget. It has been several years and a multitude of client experiences that have finally led to a completed project. I first want to acknowledge those clients who came to me with their pain and trusted me. They became my greatest teachers.

As you can imagine this endeavor doesn't happen through one's own efforts alone. The project began with the guidance and encouragement of my amazing daughter Erin. She has been my cheerleader and my *right hand man* every step of the way. Among other things, it was she who did the final edit and who came up with the brilliant idea of using QR codes to link the reader to video demonstrations of the processes in the book.

In addition I thank Leah Campbell for her astute editing, her patience with my comma obsession and her beautiful heart.

Wesley Bryant, the brilliant artist who designed my cover was a creative joy to work with. It was he who brought the angel, Nikki Edwards, into my life. She produced the book, talked me off the ledge when necessary and along with the magical talents of Doug Crowe, was instrumental in getting it successfully launched. And I thank you Chris Fore Photography for my beautiful headshot on the cover.

I have so much gratitude to the clients who fearlessly and generously gave me endorsements. I also humbly thank Michael Bernard Beckwith, John Assaraf, David Feinstein, Allison Maslan,

Ellen McCarty, Fred Gallo, George Pratt, Christina Rasmussen and Mary Sise for giving their time to look over the book and write such beautiful endorsements. I also want to thank Greg Voissen for teaching me what I needed to do, to go about getting those endorsements.

I am forever indebted to my dear friend David Hlavac for his love and encouragement to complete this much-needed book. Also on my team of male supporters, I thank my wonderful son Casey who makes me proud and always believes in me. And my gratitude to his dad, my former husband Gary, whose untimely death, along with that of my dog Sammy, inspired me to write the book.

My humble gratitude to my coaches Allison Maslan, Gina Ruby and the incredible Ellen McCarty who were there to kick my butt or calm my fears every step of the way. This completed book wouldn't have happened without you. Their support and the support of my fellow members of the Pinnacle Mastermind Group was life changing.

I thank The Association for Comprehensive Energy Psychology, on whose Board I sit, for training me and blessing me with the mind/body tools that I share in this book. My dear friends and colleagues in that organization have taken courageous steps to bring EP to the world and I am proud to be in their company.

I could not end this document without thanking my parents, Jack and Jo Gutman who have loved me and believed in me since birth, my sister Lesley who took me to my first Energy Psychology conference, and my brother Craig who is a constant source of love and encouragement. I also thank his wife Marilyn for her love and humor and their two older children Jenna, and Christopher who inspire me with their work with grieving children. Their youngest son Patrick's beautiful music compositions accompany this book and give it a soul. Thank you Dear Ones.

A single woman is nothing without her friends. My wonderful male friends have been helpful, resourceful and supportive, thank you. My *girlfriends* always give my heart wings. Their love, support and belief in me, truly sustain me. You know who you are and I love you.

And finally to all of the unseen beings who inspire and guide me every day in my work with people in emotional pain, I can honestly say...I couldn't do it without you.

I am hugely blessed and I stand in humble gratitude.

Endorsements

The Buddha captured it with poignant accuracy: "Death is that curse that makes sweet love our anguish." How do we move through that anguish and come away stronger, wiser -- even enriched -- after suffering one of life's cruelest exploits? Paula Shaw offers a guidebook that can bring precious comfort and healing. Framed within wise counsel about all the major issues involved in grieving, the book's special contribution is to expertly show you how to weave energy-healing methods into the journey.

-David Feinstein, Ph.D.
Co-Author with Peg Mayo, *Rituals for Living and Dying*
Co-Author with Donna Eden, *Energy Medicine*

Paula Shaw brings to this book 24 years of guiding people through the process of healing the grief produced by loss. Whether it is a death, job loss, identity loss, a breach of trust or faith, or the loss of a limb or physical health. Any kind of loss takes it's toll on life and most of us have no idea what to do....until now...this book shows you the way.

-John Assaraf, World Renowned Best Selling Author of *The Answer: Grow Any Business, Achieve Financial Freedom, and Live an Extraordinary Life*, CEO Neurogym

The wisdom, compassion, and skillful practices in this book are vital friends on the journey to healing from loss and grief. A most trustworthy guide, Paula Shaw has included every aspect of befriending oneself each step of the way to transforming grief into tranquility.

-Michael Bernard Beckwith

Author of *Life Visioning*

Paula Shaw has a unique gift of turning any moment into a healing moment. With a unique combination of heart and head, Paula Shaw companions grievers on the twisting, turning journey through grief.

The information and tools available in her new book, When Will This Pain Every End, will change the way you live your life forever.

-Allisan Maslan

Author of *Blast Off! The Surefire Success Plan to Launch Your Dreams Into Reality*

This book is a treasure trove of information, processes, and great journaling ideas that can effectively lead the reader to a place of resolution and healing. It is a must-have resource for every helping professional.

-Christina Rasmussen

Author of *Second Firsts--Live, Laugh and Love Again*

Paula, I do not even have words to express my gratitude. I was at the point where if someone told me to stick a knife in my hand to take away my migraines, I probably would have. The work we did and the processes we used were incredibly helpful. I am going to tell the entire world about how amazing you are.

-Atusa Palizaban, Client

First off- loving this book. It's almost funny to read it on this side of my work because it almost has more effect. Sometimes when you're in it you can't really hear, process or understand things that are being unfolded for you, but your approach and voice is so loving and clear. It feels like you're reading it to me- that may also be because I know you.

Your introduction was really touching. I feel like you so perfectly captured what happens in a child's mind when that trauma occurs. Personally, I was never able to verbalize what that internal break was. Job well done! You put it in the most humanistic terms. By that I mean even a person who was the stealer of light could read that and understand the weight of their actions, they could understand the violation in a way that would possibly force them to see themselves for what they have done.

-Edena **Hines,** Actor, Client

Loss and life are synonymous but most of us have no idea what to do when it happens to us. Paula Shaw has compiled a combination of great information with truly effective processes to help you move through loss in a growth-full, productive way. With heart and head she guides you on the perilous journey through grief. I particularly love how she instantly links you to video demonstrations of various processes in the book through QR codes. Brilliant!

-George J. Pratt Ph.D
Former Chairman, Psychology
Scripps Memorial Hospital, La Jolla, CA
Co-Author, *Code to Joy*

When I recently experienced the sudden and tragic loss of a young family member, I found myself in a place I had never been before with grief. I was utterly incapable of processing as a mother myself, how one goes on with the loss of your child. When I reached out to Paula Shaw, I literally couldn't care or think about stages of grief, or even processing it... What I needed immediately was so simple, yet so very vital.

What do I say to her Mother (my Cousin who is a Sister to me) following her daughter's burial? I simply and desperately needed the right words! I was terrified I would say something that would send her further into retreat and isolation during this agonizing time.

Paula knew exactly what to say. I was able to immediately reach out to my cousin with confidence, opening our conversation with one of Paula's suggestions...just a phrase, a few words...that was all we needed. I didn't have to say another word from there. The floodgates opened and all she needed was to be heard. Paula even taught me what not to say, and I am forever grateful. A lot of what my cousin has shared is about how misunderstood and alone she feels, and how others comments and attempts to reach out—do cause her additional upset, frustration, deeper grief, and even anger—though she knows they had the best intentions.

I cannot thank you enough, Paula, for the healing you implement and the work that you do!

-Ellen McCarty
Master Coach, AMI

Paula Shaw changed the course of my life one morning in April 2010. I was told that morning that my marriage of 29 ½ years was over. It was a devastating blow, and there was no room for discussion.

Paula, who knew us both, began to work her magic. We discussed the idea that "as one door closes, another one opens". That mental image, as well as other modalities she showed me, allowed me to move forward seeking open doors, rather than dwelling on the closed door behind me. Focusing on the positive (as hard as that was) allowed me to move on, and with some work, with an attitude of gratitude, I created a new life. She let me read the first chapters of this book and I couldn't wait to see the completed version.

Thank you Paula for being the angel that delivered the perfect message at the perfect time!

-Tim Scanlon, Client

In "When Will this Pain Ever End?", Paula Shaw offers us an amazing grief-relieving manual for transitioning from pain and loss to relief and wellbeing. She guides us through a precision and heartfelt tour that clears the way for suffering to be truly optional by learning how to suffer well, by tapping into happiness at the same time. Integrated with helpful videos, the methods covered are easily and effectively applied to get beneficial results.

-Fred P. Gallo PhD

ACEP President

Author of *Energy Psychology, and Energy Tapping for Trauma*

Using the knowledge and experiential exercises in this book the reader will be able to move from the depths of grief to the preciousness of life itself.

-Mary Sise, LCSW

Co-Author, *The Energy of Belief: Psychology's Power Tools to Focus Intention & Release Blocking Beliefs*

My appreciation and gratitude for Paula are abundant. During the time I have been her client, she has helped me through numerous, unfortunate, tumultuous times. She not only hears my concerns and issues she provides me with helpful, coping tools and solutions on a consistent basis. I attribute my ability to conquer my hardships, to the support and guidance of Paula. I am eternally grateful for the blessing of this woman.

-Michelle MacDonald, Client

I originally sought Paula's help a few years back to overcome a lifelong fear of suffocation. Within a few sessions I was able to be rational in situations that had previously left me in a full-blown panic. More recently, I got into a bad pattern of consuming alcohol in inappropriate situations and amounts. Weekly sessions with Paula over the past 2 months has not only changed that pattern through uncovering unconscious beliefs from my childhood as well as triggers in my current situation, it has also given me more clarity in some of the major aspects of my life.

In sessions, Paula uses a combination of different energy healing modalities, muscle testing, intuition, chakra balancing and good old verbal counseling. She is an excellent listener, has an uncanny ability to ask just the right questions, and gives very constructive feedback. She is professional, empathetic and caring, and it is easy for me to open up and share with her anything that is on my mind, without fear of being judged. With her counsel, I have overcome obstacles in life that I couldn't seem to conquer on my own, and I am truly grateful for all the ways she has helped me create a healthier, happier and more fulfilling life.

-Tina Ostbo, Client

PAULA SHAW

Table of Contents

Introduction

Crying, Waiting, Hoping

"Crying, waiting, hoping you'll come back"

The Beatles (*Crying, Waiting, Hoping*)

"From time to time, life shakes us up, twirling or even destroying the foundation we've built. Such an experience can be quite disorienting—and it is supposed to be. The purpose of change beyond our control is to shake us up so we must hasten in a new direction.

Like the soul that has left the body of the deceased, we may not be able to find our way back to our past base. But the past is dead, and there is no reason to return. We are free to move on to discover a new life in a new world. Upheaval is a gift of love. When it comes, ask to see the blessing in what you're being forced to release, to make way for something new and better."

Allen Cohen, *A Deep Breath of Life*

If you are reading this book, you have known pain. You may be experiencing a deep brokenness right now, and wondering, *"When will this pain ever end?"* Perhaps you fear this agony is a life sentence, that it will be impossible for you to know joy again. It's a dark, sinking feeling, devoid of hope. I've been there, and have known that fear. That's why I decided to write this book, to let you know that your pain doesn't have to last forever, no matter how it may appear right now.

Many of you who pick up this book will be suffering the loss of a loved one, but grief is not just a response to death; it is the normal, natural response to any kind of loss. All loss creates grief, and loss comes in many shapes and sizes.

My first encounter with grief came unexpectedly around the age of five. My grandfather, who was a Merchant Marine, had docked in a nearby port and was to stay with us for a few days. This was exciting because he traveled all over the world and always brought us glamorous, exotic presents when he came to visit. I still remember a musical jewelry box with a spinning ballerina that he brought me from Japan. It was a cherished possession for years. However, on this occasion, something happened that would change my life dramatically and introduce me to loss and grief.

I don't know where my brother and sister had gone, but for some reason they were not home. My mother was in the kitchen cooking dinner and I was alone with my grandfather in another room. One of the things we kids loved so much about him, was that he would always play games with us. On this particular day, however, a game that began with tickling ended in sexual abuse. All I can remember is being confused, scared, and feeling sick inside. Because everybody loved him so much and thought he was such a great guy, I was sure there was something wrong with me that had made the bad thing happen. I was too ashamed and afraid of that dark thing inside me to tell anyone what had happened, so I kept it secret until I was 21 years old.

Enmeshed in that confusion, during my teenage years, I interpreted the normal *come on* behaviors of adolescent guys as the result of the badness in me, making them do bad things. I was terrified to reveal this ugly truth about myself to anyone, so there was no opportunity to correct my misguided thinking. It wasn't until many years later, in therapy, that I learned I was the victim of a sick man; that there had been no darkness or evil in me...only an innocent child who had been abused and bewildered by an inappropriate adult act.

There might not have been a death in the family, but on that afternoon, at five years of age, I suffered huge loss. The loss of my innocence and self-confidence, loss of trust in my grandfather, loss of faith that my parents would keep me safe, loss of my belief that I was a good girl, that God loved me and I would go to heaven, and so many other losses I can't even name. My world was turned upside down and I officially became a griever; and like all grievers, I was destabilized, scared, and had no idea what to do. This experience, and the secret keeping I engaged in, led to years of me being attracted to abusive, emotionally unavailable, narcissistic men, and to circumstances that were not in line with my highest good. In spite of (or perhaps as a result of) my mastery of co-dependent behavior, my relationships with men didn't go well.

After two marriages and two divorces, another huge grief episode occurred, which again changed my life dramatically. During the summer of 2008, my former husband and father of my children (with whom I had remained very close), and our family dog of 14 years, died suddenly, within a month of each other. It was a very dark time for me, and for my two young adult children. By this time I was a therapist, with specialty training in Grief Counseling and Energy Psychology work. I had focused on grief work at the beginning of my career, but had put it to the side when I discovered the exciting world of Energy Psychology, the processes of which could help people make huge shifts in a relatively short time, compared to traditional therapy. While I loved both these areas of work, I had not combined them because I thought grief was too monumental to be helped by Mind/Body methods, which seemed so simple.

However, I was now faced with two children for whom I was the sole parent, and clients who depended on me. I needed to be back on my feet and functioning, and I was ready to do whatever I needed to do. In a desperate attempt to heal myself as rapidly as I could, I combined what I knew about grief work with the processes of Energy Psychology. The results were profound, so much so that the tools that guided me through my transformation – and the transformation of countless others I have helped since – have become the contents of this book.

Two months later, I sat in my office with a devastated client who had just lost his dog the week before. I told him, "I don't know exactly how you feel but I have a pretty good idea, because I recently lost my dog, too."

"How long ago?" he asked.

When I told him, he looked at me incredulously; I clearly seemed fine. "Are you on meds?" he wondered.

I chuckled and replied, "No, I'm not."

He stared at me in disbelief and asked, "How did you do it?"

That question is what led me to write this book. It made me realize I needed to compile the tools, information and processes that worked so well for me and share them with you.

There *is* a way out. All you need to do is be clear that you want things to be different, and then make the decision to walk with me through each step outlined in this book. Take it slowly and be consistent; do a little something every day. Most importantly, don't be afraid. Even when it seems impossible, there *is* a way forward from grief. I found it, and so can you.

A Personal Introduction from Paula

To view this video, simply scan the QR code with a QR Code Reader App on your Smart Phone or Tablet. If you do not have one, simply visit the app store and search: QR Code Reader. Or you can visit YouTube.com/user/PaulaShawCounseling, Go to Playlist > When Will This Pain Ever End? Introduction

Introduction

I'm A Loser

"Although I laugh and I act like a clown, beneath this mask I am

wearing a frown."

The Beatles (*I'm A Loser*)

When we are dealing with pain and grief it is often exhausting, so I understand that you may feel that you are incapable of any effort at all. Don't worry. This isn't boot camp. Remember, I have been where you are.

Throughout this book, I will be gently guiding you through processes and information that I know will help you. But at each step, you will decide how much you are able to do. You won't need to read every page and you will always be encouraged to go at your own pace. Only you know the right way for you to grieve and I will not presume to be the expert on your pain.

Let's be clear, there are **no stages** that you *must* go through and there isn't a required list of feelings that you *must* experience in order to heal. This is your loss and your pain. I am simply offering an assemblage of information and processes that have worked for me, and my clients, over twenty-four years of practice. Sift through what I have to offer and find what feels right for you.

Loss and Change

We humans hate loss and change, really any kind of variation from the norm. Yet from the moment we lose the tranquility of the womb and enter the confusion and upheaval of birth, loss and change are part of our lives. Since the normal, human response to this unexpected turbulence is usually protest, is it any wonder that a baby's first act is to cry?

A possession, a partner, a place, an image of self, or a sense of security suddenly gone; this all creates change, loss, and the inevitable discomfort with the unfamiliar.

Even when we are looking forward to a change or transition, such as a new marriage, it still comes coupled with loss. The loss of living as a single person, loss of focus on ourselves, and loss of what we once knew. And that loss creates disorientation and emotional pain. We often call that pain grief, but grief is really more of a genre than an emotion.

Grief comes in many flavors and sizes. It can show up as unstoppable tears, exhaustion or anxiety, fear or reclusiveness. It can manifest as an inability to focus, or an inexplicable pervasive sadness. It can morph itself into addiction and depression. And grief, my friends, resulting from loss, is an inevitable part of life.

Sound discouraging? It doesn't have to. This book is about shifting. It's about moving forward and finding the direction that will eventually take you back to joy. A life transition doesn't have to be a life sentence of pain, but it does take deliberate, committed action to find a way out.

The obvious next question would be, "What kind of action do we take?" It's a good question and the sad truth is that most people don't know the answer. They have no idea what to do. They don't teach this in school. So how do we know what kinds of actions are productive and which are destructive?

A further complication we must deal with is that a good deal of the time, people don't even realize that they are traversing the landscape of grief. Only with something very obvious, like the death of someone they loved, are they cognitive of what they are in the middle of. Most don't realize that their depression, anxiety, eating disorders, alcoholism, or inability to maintain relationships might very likely be the result of a loss they experienced and didn't come to peace with.

What I have found to be true is that when we have good tools and we use them, it becomes possible for our pain to act as a catalyst for important change.

Losses and life transitions seem to come in two genres. Author Barrie Davenport calls these groups: *the Slow Growers* and *the Surprise Attackers*.

Some examples of Slow Growers would be things like puberty, menopause, reaching adulthood, empty-nesting, career change, relationship changes, or retirement.

The Surprise Attackers are more intense and sudden. These would be experiences like death, job loss, divorce or a relationship ending, a serious illness, an affair, unexpected moves, natural disasters or financial upheaval.

In this book, we will explore seven dimensions or phases that are present in every loss experience. Let me emphasize that these are ***not*** stages that you have to go through in order to heal, but rather aspects of the journey through loss and grief that most people will experience. Everyone won't experience all of them, nor will they experience them to the same degree. They simply exist, and traversing each of them, as fully as possible is desirable if you are to move through your emotional pain in a growth-filled and productive manner.

As your guide, I will provide you with additional articles that I wrote over the years for my *Beyond Loss* grief support group. They contain in-depth information about different features of this grief journey. I'll suggest helpful actions for you to take and give you processes to assist you in working through the pain and upheaval that naturally occurs during these times. As I said, you don't need to do everything offered. Let your intuition guide you to do what feels right for you.

One note of emphasis: expressing your feelings is critical. If we openly express painful feelings from the onset of the loss, eventually the intensity dulls and healing begins. But few of us allow ourselves this natural progression. We have lives. We have things to do and we can't let anything stop us. So we find a way to either access what we think is the fast track through the emotional pain, or we try to avoid it altogether.

It is the goal of my work to help people accept and experience their normal, natural responses to pain and stop trying to hide and disguise them.

Today we are fortunate to have proven, cutting edge, mind/body approaches that can help people get through these experiences and heal far more rapidly and productively than ever before. I have used these tools multiple times over the years in seemingly hopeless situations and watched them transform lives over and over again. So, if you have found yourself asking, "When will this pain ever end?" just keep reading and do the suggested work. These are processes that have been highly effective for thousands of people in emotional pain and they can also work for you.

CHAPTER TWO

Do You Want to Know a Secret?

"Listen, do you want to know a secret?"

The Beatles (*Do You Want to Know a Secret?*)

The Body/Mind Solution

It's actually no secret anymore. Quantum Physics has taught us all that, "Everything is Energy!" That means everything, your thoughts, your behaviors, your skin, your hair, your pain...it's all energy vibrating at different frequencies. So when a behavior or a feeling becomes problematic, the best thing we can do is isolate the frequency, intervene on it and neutralize it. Although it sounds like something out of a Sci-Fi movie, we can actually do this easily with the tools of Energy Psychology and Energy Medicine. Doesn't it make logical sense that the best way to heal dysfunctional energy patterns, is with Energy Medicine?

The miraculous methods that have been created within the energy compendium can help even devastated grievers shift to a place where they can begin to take healing steps and implement healing behaviors into their lifestyles. It is imperative that we explore and employ successful methods from these fields because we know that when loss goes unaddressed, both body and mind become vulnerable. Life transitions and loss go hand in hand, but loss and illness don't have to be inseparable companions as well.

The Buddha warned us long ago, that, "life is suffering". But I think what he really meant was, life is full of change and change embodies loss. When we don't know how to deal with loss, we suffer.

Emotional pain can be grueling when we have no tools for dealing with the devastating feelings it generates; feelings such as anguish, anger, fear, despair, hopelessness and a terrifying loss of control. These feelings are difficult and frightening. No one wants to go through this kind of agony, yet we must feel it and walk through it, not avoid it, if we are to heal productively.

The tools and processes offered here will help you to manage and lessen your pain, so you will be better able to move through your losses and life transitions in a growth-filled, illuminating way.

Let me explain this more thoroughly with a story that illustrates how finding the energetic root of emotional pain, combined with the use of powerful Energy Psychology tools, created a profound transformation with one of my clients, who I'll call Lynn. She telephoned me one afternoon following the breakup of her three-year relationship. The CEO of a large, successful company, she had been in bed for days and was now rendered completely unable to function.

She lamented that she was devastated, couldn't eat, didn't seem to care about anything and even said she felt like she wanted to die. Lynn confessed that she had broken up with men before and had never had a reaction like this one. She even confided in me that she was more functional after the death of her mother.

After talking for a bit, I began to see that the recent breakup had triggered an old wound, which had been created by sexual abuse from a trusted family member. Long ago, this betrayal had set up a belief in her that the men she loved would always betray her. Like so many abused children, she had no opportunity to get help to process and heal that betrayal. Later, other experiences of betrayal in adolescence and adulthood cemented that negative belief even further.

When she fell in love with the man in question, she thought all the betrayal was behind her. Because she was so happy, she let her guard down and trusted him. Imagine the devastation she felt when she found out that he had cheated on her. Although he said it meant nothing to him, it meant everything to her. Once more, the belief, that she would always be betrayed by men she loved, had reared its ugly head. She now felt doomed to live this nightmare over and over. This was the core of what had paralyzed her with emotional pain.

Through using some of the mind/body tools I will introduce to you later, such as Setting Intention and Meridian Tapping, she was able to neutralize the betrayal belief that was central to her devastation. Robbed of its power, this belief was no longer able to drain her energy and zap her hope. Nor was it any longer able to attract life experiences that validated its accuracy.

From this point, we did some additional work on the loss and she quickly returned to a fully functioning life. This was actually done in two sessions. It doesn't always happen that rapidly, but more often than not, measurable change can occur from the very first session when using the tools of Energy Psychology and other Mind/Body approaches.

Before we get into the nitty-gritty of loss, change and challenge, we need to look at the part that energy plays. It is because of this central role that mind/body tools work so well. They are designed to address problems effectively at their energetic point of origin. As a member of the Board of the Association for Comprehensive Energy Psychology, my goal is to expose as many people as possible to the wonderful tools of this field. I will be sharing many of them in the chapters that follow.

My private practice is part of the Center for Age Management medical practice in San Diego, California. My colleague, Dr. Andrea Cole, and I both consider health to be a balancing act that involves the body and the mind. When she refers someone to me who is dealing with both physical and emotional issues, the first thing I do is what I call the "Historical Dig."

This is a process in which the client and I review life experiences and I look for the transitions, losses and subsequent unhealed emotional pain that inevitably lead to the creation of dysfunctional beliefs and energy patterns. These culprits are usually at the origin of the existing condition. More often than not, a loss occurred long ago but went unrecognized and unaddressed. This unhealed emotional pain sets up the perfect *Petri dish* in which to grow the components of physical illness and emotional dysfunction.

In their best-selling book, **Code To Joy,** my friends, Drs. George Pratt and Peter Lambrou explain the concept of *micro-traumas.* Micro-traumas are negative experiences that we might not have even realized impacted us in a traumatic way. Even without that awareness, though, they made an indelible imprint that deepened over the years. An example of a micro-trauma and it's resulting outcome might be an embarrassing incident that happened while speaking in front of a class in school, that, over the years, lead to a permanent fear of public speaking.

In agreement, I must say that it is rare when some level of traumatic circumstance fails to be present in chronic physical illness and emotional dysfunction. Time and time again, the patients who have come to Dr. Cole for a physical ailment, end up in my office dealing with the unfaithful partner, the unfair job-loss or the childhood parental abuse that created the emotional component that led to the heart problem, the ulcer, or what ever other issue they originally sought her out to heal.

The Body/Mind Connection

The understanding of this mental/emotional/physical connection had its beginning over 2000 years ago. There are ancient writings connecting powerful emotions like anger, grief and sadness with illness. But more recently in the 1970's, O. Carl Simonton M.D. published work and spoke prolifically on the connection between grief and the onset of cancer. In the majority of the patients studied, cancer was linked with a significant loss experienced six months to a year before the cancer appeared.

Dr. Elilda Evans published, *A Psychological Study of Cancer* (1926), in which she reported that in an analysis of one hundred cancer patients, the majority of those patients had lost an important emotional relationship before the onset of the disease. She saw these patients as people who had invested their identity in another individual, an object or role, rather than developing their own individuality based on a strong sense of self. When the object or role was threatened or removed, such patients were thrown back on themselves, with few internal resources to cope.

In *The Type C Connection,* —Lydia Temoshak Ph.D. & Henry Dreker, further explore the association between cancer and repressed emotions:

> *"Primary emotions like anger, fear, and sadness do not have any harmful effect on our bodies. They alter our physiology, but so does every natural biological function. It's only when we habitually block feelings, that they become toxic states that are closely associated with weakened immunity."*

Dr. Candace Pert Ph.D. offers another perspective in her landmark, cutting edge book, *Molecules of Emotion*:

"My research has shown me that when emotions are expressed—which is to say that the bio-chemicals that are substrate of emotion are flowing freely—all systems are united and whole. When emotions are repressed, denied, not allowed to be whatever they may be, our network pathways get blocked, stopping the flow of the vital feel-good, unifying chemicals that run both our biology and our behavior."

Pert felt that emotions, which up to now have been largely ignored within the traditional confines of science and medicine, might actually be the key to understanding psycho-immunology's emerging picture of how body and mind affect each other.

For example, it's through the emotion-modulating peptides that an embarrassing thought can cause blood vessels to dilate and turn a face beet red. In the same way, the molecules of emotion can mobilize immune cells to destroy an incipient tumor. Techniques like meditation or visualization may also act as forces to set those molecules in action, as physiological changes have been scientifically documented when engaging in both of these activities.

The Body/Mind Solution

Much of the current research available to us is supporting the idea of a body-mind connection, so doesn't it make perfect sense that a body-mind problem needs a body-mind solution?

The word *emotion* actually comes from the Latin root meaning "to move." The very name of the thing is telling us how to deal with it. We are supposed to move through our painful feelings, not become them!

It is so tempting to wish that we could bypass experiencing and moving through life's agonies. God knows that many people try to do this through the distractions of work, substances or addictive behaviors. But avoiding pain doesn't dissipate the energy of it. If we aren't willing to experience the pain and process through it, we are opening the door to a myriad of problems.

Unhealed emotional pain can linger like a low-grade fever, waiting for some unknown event to ignite it into a life-threatening inferno. It can also go underground, lurking beneath the surface, wreaking havoc from the inside out through physical or emotional illness. Fortunately, or unfortunately, in the words of the old saying, "The only way out is through."

So if you are open to taking the journey, let's explore seven phases or dimensions that naturally occur when one is experiencing loss and life transitions. They don't necessarily happen in a specific order for everyone, but if you want to heal productively, it is wise to consciously navigate and master these dimensions.

In my research I discovered that moving from the body's Root Center up, there is a progressive connection between the energy of each center and a particular phase of the journey through loss. It's interesting to note that these energy centers are associated with the major glands and nerve bundles of the human body. Each one represents different aspects of the mind/body/spirit connection. We will look at this in more depth in the next chapter.

Don't worry, while there is a great deal of information here, you can work with it in small chunks. All I ask is that you show up for yourself every day and walk toward your goal of being healed, healthy and vibrant again. Every action you take will get you closer to that end. Some days you will be able to do more than others...that's okay, it's human. Just keep doing something, a little something every day. That is what will make the difference. The natural state of energy is to move and expand. If you don't give it a place to go, it will just circle itself and you'll get stuck.

Over the years I have seen amazing outcomes happen again and again. That's exactly why I felt it was so important to compile these powerful tools and information. My hope is that they will be of as much assistance to you as they have been to others who were going through loss and change with no idea how to bring the pain to an end. Will it still hurt? Of course it will, but not as much and not for as long.

I close with these beautiful words by Peg Elliott Mayo (from *Rituals for Living and Dying,* a book she co-authored with David Feinstein):

> *"The terrible fire of grief is an energetic furnace, refining character, personality, intellect and soul. It is a catalyst for creation.*
>
> *What is created may be dreadful--A distorted unapproachable monument to despair-- or a distillation of experience that is wholesome, useful, bright, and even wise."*

CHAPTER THREE

Help!

"Help me get my feet back on the ground.

Won't you please, please help me?"

The Beatles (*Help!*)

The Energy: Explosive, Primal, Survival-Oriented – Relating to the body's Root Energy Center

The Action: Express Your Initial Intense, Chaotic, and Volatile Feelings

The emotions experienced during this initial phase, when the shock first hits you, are primal. Whether your urges are to scream, cry, beat on pillows, or swear like a sailor; the painful, negative energy needs to be released. This kind of Energy is intense and chaotic and needs to be dissipated or it can become a toxic force within you. This is best done by feeling the feelings and expressing them as fully and as authentically as possible. This is the time when the intensity of the pain will drive you to wail, "When will this pain ever end?"

Releasing this energy may involve screaming from the rooftops, doubling over in tearful agony, pounding on the table, kick boxing, running, bike riding or any other dynamic means of releasing the intense energy rising up within you in protest to the upheaval you're experiencing.

It is also possible, however, that you might experience a quieter expression of these initial feelings. You may find yourself softly sobbing, spending time in quiet reflection, listening to your inner voice, praying or meditating. More commonly however, when some kind of life transition creates turmoil and loss, the primary energy experienced is intense, powerful and frequently out of control.

After the initial outcry, it is more likely that the quieter feelings will come to the forefront. We might become sad, anxious or depressed, in short, more subdued. This enables us to function better in our everyday lives and social interactions, but doesn't necessarily help us to heal.

Many of us only associate loss and its subsequent grief with death, and don't understand that loss is so much bigger than that one manifestation. Loss is any experience of having a treasured person, place, relationship, or object removed from your life. Any life transition fits this description.

It is emotionally painful to no longer be able to hug, hold or talk to that special someone. It hurts when we no longer have our animals to pet, cherish and love. We don't like to move our homes or offices and we want our bodies to always stay perfect, high functioning and youthful. We hate change and yet without it, life gets stale and boring. This ancient battle between our need for change and our love of the familiar is a central core of the human dilemma.

When you experience a loss, everything turns upside down and life as you knew it ceases to exist. Underneath the surface of any incident, there is the loss of one or all of the following:

- Hopes and Dreams,
- Trust
- Life Circumstances

The Energy Story

All emotions, behaviors, thoughts and feelings are simply energy vibrating at different frequencies and all energy is mutable. It can be changed, and that change can lead to healing. As we saw in the last chapter, once the energy is shifted, miraculous healing is possible.

This truth legitimately creates the hope that it is possible to be liberated from our anger, fear, sadness, anxiety, physical illness, and the addictions that serve as distractions from our pain. However, we must take action if we are to heal. We often think that because loss and change are normal aspects of life, we should be able to get over them naturally and move on quickly.

Most of the time, however, it isn't that easy because we aren't just dealing with the situation in front of us. We are dealing with an accumulation of un-healed emotional pain that has built up over a lifetime. For this reason, it becomes necessary to take conscious, deliberate action if we are to heal productively and eventually accept the new normal in our lives - a normal in which life is different but is also potentially richer and more abundant with joy, gratitude and wisdom.

The energy that animates us and gives us life is stored within our bodies in Energy Centers, sometimes called Chakras. It is then run throughout our bodies through the Meridians, which are the lines of energy utilized in acupuncture. Their functioning is very similar to the relationship between the heart and the veins.

I have found it interesting that the seven phases, or dimensions, that we encounter when working through life transitions, tie in with each of the seven major energy centers.

- The Root Center connects to the primal, chaotic energy of the "Why Me?" moment when loss first occurs.

- The Sacral Center connects to the relationship energy and the need for comfort and support from others.

- The Solar Plexus Center connects to the self and the need for self-focus and self-care.

- The Heart Center connects to the expression of feelings, which is central in processing through loss.

- The Throat Center connects to the need to speak one's truth about what is being felt and experienced.

- The Brow Center connects to the confused thinking that initially takes place, eventually giving way to wiser new kinds of thinking as one heals and begins to enter living in the new normal.

- Finally, the Crown Center connects to the spiritual processes that help us heal and ultimately, give service to others.

We don't necessarily experience the dimensions in any set progression (from Root Center to Crown Center). But still, in the productive, healthy processing of our emotions, all of these dimensions will likely be experienced.

The Root Center Energy

If you are in the initial stage of a life transition, you are probably experiencing raw, primal emotions that result in behaviors such as wailing, sobbing and screaming. You may feel as though your very survival is threatened. These emotions are intense, chaotic and deeply felt. These kinds of feelings relate to the Root Center, the base of self-preservation. Family legacy, traditions and beliefs, connection to the Earth and to one's country, all relate to this energy center.

This is where it all begins. This is where the "Why God?" moments are experienced. The sense that you can't live through this is felt here in the first phase. It is important to allow expression of these intense emotions. Suppressing feelings of this magnitude can be harmful. It is best to let it rip. Let the intensity of the feelings move through and out of you. Most of the time, the news of the loss or the first knowing of it is a shock. And shock causes emotional upheaval. This emotional state is naturally accompanied by sounds. Loud sounds. To try to behave in any other way is un-natural.

However, too often our life circumstances don't allow our responses to the shock to be as intense as they actually are. Instead, we have to consider the time, the place and the people involved and try to taper our responses to be appropriate to them.

Let me sum it up this way. The Root is a basic, primal survival oriented center. Set social graces aside and emote fully, honestly and genuinely. That is the healthiest thing you can do. The Rant, a process I later recommend, will help you to do just that. It is my experience that you can't come to a place of calm and some level of acceptance until you fully express and process the intense, core shaking, initial feelings. After this has taken place, one can begin to have alone, meditative time to contemplate the realities of the loss. Trying to be calm and composed before expression of the shock and chaos, usually leads to complications. It is putting the cart before the horse.

Each step of the way, you will be given important, informative pieces to read and suggested journaling to assist with healing and awareness. You will also find cutting edge Energy Medicine/Energy Psychology processes to help you shift the energy, while healing and attaining readiness for the next aspect of the journey. If you don't feel ready to do any of the processes, read on and come back to them when you do.

Read:

The Dimensions of Grief Energy (pg. 39) and Am I Crazy? (pg. 50)

Processes to Do:

The Rant (pg. 60), Square Breathing (pg. 63) and Balanced Breathing (pg. 64). Root Center Balancers, (pg. 66) EFT (pg. 67).

Square Breathing   Balanced Breathing

EFT

Journal:

Express the intense, difficult feelings that you are experiencing. This isn't about award winning journalism, so swear, rant and scream...it's all good! Those feelings are definitely better out than in. Let it out. You're probably mad as hell, or devastated, and you get to say so. As you progress through the book, always feel free to write about whatever feels important to you. My suggestions are just a guideline. The most important thing is that you are engaged in a process of personal insight and expression.

Chapter Three Articles

The Dimensions of Grief Energy

The emotions produced by grief are varied and unpredictable. Everyone's experience is unique. A significant loss or transition affects your head, your heart, and your spirit. The emotions it produces do not occur in orderly stages, as is so often misunderstood. Elizabeth Kubler-Ross taught us about the stages of death and dying, and unfortunately these stages have been misinterpreted as being the same for the grieving loved ones left behind.

Rather than stages, grief more accurately happens in dimensions or phases. These dimensions are usually experienced in waves, some small, some huge; some dimensions you will never experience at all. The most important thing to remember is that they do not come in any particular order!

SHOCK, DENIAL, NUMBNESS, DISBELIEF

These emotions are the protectors, the insulators, keeping you from the full reality of the loss until you are more ready to accept it. They may last only a short time, or they may stay longer. This constellation of dazed, stunned feelings will be more intense if the loss was totally unexpected. However, even if it was expected, the feeling of being in a fog, of being there, but not there, will be experienced to some degree. These emotions may manifest themselves in hysterical crying, outbursts of anger, laughter, or staring off into space.

If we were to look at an energetic perspective of this dimension, it would be synonymous with a shut down of the Heart Center. The overload of emotions would cause blowout of the energy circuits of the Heart Center and the result would look like a dazed, disoriented and disconnected being.

DISORGANIZATION, CONFUSION, SEARCHING, YEARNING

After a significant loss, it is normal to feel a sense of restlessness, agitation, impatience and ongoing confusion. It's like being in the middle of a raging river, unable to get a grasp onto anything. Disconnected thoughts race through your mind and strong emotions overwhelm you. It may become difficult to complete any task due to confusion, disorganization and forgetfulness. Early morning and late at night can be especially difficult. At these times disorientation, fatigue, hopelessness, confusion, and lack of initiative can be especially strong. Often experienced is a restless searching for the person who is gone. Yearning can become so strong, that you actually think that you see the person on the street, or hear them coming into the house. Another part of this emotional dimension is experiencing visual hallucinations. You may have a real sense of the person's presence, or catch a fleeting glimpse of them across the room. This is not abnormal! You are not crazy!

Energetically, we are seeing a Brow Center breakdown and shut down. When what we have to contemplate on a cognitive level is the unthinkable, we are unable to function in a normal, rational way.

Other common experiences at this time will be difficulties with sleeping, loss of appetite, or overeating. Dreaming of the person who has been lost is a very normal thing to do. Embrace the pleasant dreams and be careful not to over-interpret the unpleasant ones. While these dimensions of grief can be strange, they are normal and necessary. Following a loss, disorganization precedes reorientation.

ANXIETY, PANIC, FEAR

As the realities of life set in, anxiety can increase. These feelings are a perfectly natural response to the trauma and upheaval experienced following a loss.

Questions like, "How will I survive?" "Will my life ever have meaning again?" "How will I tell the children?" will naturally come up in a swell of panic and fear. Financial concerns, housing changes, parenting worries and other such "real life stuff," can exacerbate this emotional dimension. Your energy is drained and you can easily feel overwhelmed. It is critical at this time to talk these fears over with someone safe. Processing them will help to keep them from growing into real problems of their own. Isolating, feeling shame, and keeping them to yourself, is a sure way to give them the power they need to grow and become detrimental.

These basic, survival-oriented thoughts are integrally connected with the body's Root Center - the center concerned with survival, and connection to family, country and other central connections.

PHYSIOLOGICAL CHANGES

You may be shocked at how strongly your body responds to the impact of a loss. One of the most prevalent problem areas is sleep. Many people have difficulty getting to sleep. Others wake up in the night and can't get back to sleep. Sleeping normally is an act of giving up control. When you experience a severe loss, you feel a loss of control. The need to stay awake sometimes relates to the fear of additional losses occurring while you are asleep and out of control.

Another contributing factor to an inability to sleep may be fears of overwhelming painful thoughts and feelings that might be expressed through dreams, or fears of being alone in bed if you are not used it. The truly frustrating factor is that your body needs more rest than usual when you are grieving, and being unable to sleep well leaves you feeling tired most of the time.

Other physical manifestations of your grief can be muscle aches and pains, shortness of breath, feelings of emptiness in your stomach, tightness in your throat or chest, digestive problems, sensitivity to noise, heart palpitations, queasiness, nausea, headaches, increased allergic reactions, changes in appetite, weight loss or gain, agitation and generalized tension. Should any of these symptoms be part of your grief journey, don't be overly alarmed. The key is to take good care of your body. With proper nurturing it will heal as you do the work of grieving. Remember, however, to listen to your body. If it tells you that something is really seriously wrong, see a physician. Give yourself whatever peace of mind you can.

There is an important energy center that is not one of the major seven, it is called the Thymus

Center and it is very involved with the immune system. When this center is challenged, we can begin to experience physical breakdown. What is experienced in this dimension connects with the Thymus Center and the Brow Center.

EXPLOSIVE EMOTIONS

Some people feel more comfortable expressing explosive emotions than they feel expressing the pain, helplessness, fear, and hurt that are actually underneath them. This can be particularly true for men. Society as a whole still tends to discourage or censor explosive emotions. We need to remember that these emotions are not good or bad, right or wrong. They may not be logical, but they are real, and we are just as entitled to feel them, as we are any other emotions we may have.

One of the most common feelings in this dimension is anger at God. This is very real and very painful, yet incredibly difficult to express, due to deeply ingrained fears of condemnation by the church, society, or even God.

There are two ways to express your explosive emotions, outwardly and inwardly. Outward expression will lead to healing; inward expression can lead to the creation of even greater problems. This doesn't mean that it is okay to go around screaming, raging, and abusing people in your life. To express outwardly in a productive way, you must find a safe person or persons, with whom you can express your feelings before they build up into destructive explosions.

This is not always easy to do because there is so much societal pressure to repress explosive emotions. However, repression is a dangerous path to walk, because explosive emotions turned inward can lead to chronic feelings of low self-esteem, depression, guilt, physical conditions and even persistent thoughts of suicide. An important thing to remember about these emotions is that they are a normal and important part of the grief journey. Like all the other dimensions of the journey, if we are to heal, we must accept them, experience them, and express them.

These emotions, while connected to the Heart Center, also deeply connect to the Solar Plexus Center, which is the center concerned with the Self. These emotions have at their core a fear and concern of, "What will happen to me?" This survival-based kind of thinking also connects to the Root Center. There is nothing wrong with this kind of thinking. Under the circumstances, it is very normal. But it is painful and scary and we don't want it to persist.

GUILT AND REGRET

Most of the time when we think we feel guilt, what we are really experiencing is a wish that things had been different, or better. Real, justifiable guilt following a loss is a rare occurrence. Even if we regret an action later, we were usually doing the best we could with the level of growth and consciousness we had at the time.

Guilt is more about knowing the correct course of action, and making a conscious choice to act otherwise. This is very different from thinking at the time that a given action was correct, only to learn through time and experience that it was a mistake. There are, however, some very real feelings of guilt that arise for some people, and it is important to acknowledge and express them. Don't let someone intellectualize you out of your right to the full spectrum of your feelings. There are a few categories of guilt that are commonly experienced, which we will briefly review.

The person left alive after someone they love has died commonly experiences Survival Guilt. This would also be common for survivors of an accident or natural disaster. As with all other feelings, it is critical to find someone to talk it out with.

Relief-guilt Syndrome occurs when you feel relief after the loss of someone in your life. This is common when someone has been ill for a long time, or when there have been unpleasant aspects of the relationship that you are relieved are over.

Some people have felt guilty about things all their lives, which we call Chronic Guilt, as a personality aspect. This often begins in childhood, where a normal aspect of development is to feel responsible for causing all things, good and bad, to happen. These people take on far more guilt than is appropriate and should seek professional help to understand and change this behavior.

Magical thinking and guilt occurs when a person has at some time wished someone gone, dead, hurt or some other such negative outcome, and then it happens. This can be especially devastating for adolescents who are still somewhat susceptible to their natural magical thinking. Their situation gets even more complicated as a result of the normal developmental tasks of rebellion and individuation. All relationships have periods when problems and negative thoughts occur. Your mind, however, doesn't have the power to inflict death or some other tragic occurrence on another person. It will be critical for the person caught in this type of guilt to express these feelings to a compassionate, safe person.

When a person has done a great deal of the work of mourning and begins to re-enter life, they may experience Joy-guilt Syndrome. Experiencing joy again can bring up feelings of guilt or disloyalty to the person who is gone. We often have the misconceived idea that our pain is a kind of monument to the love and loyalty we felt for the person lost. Suffering is not an expression of love; it is an expression of pain. It is normal and healthy to reach a point where a person feels alive again, and becomes desirous of new relationships. If this kind of guilt comes up, it is important to talk it out so that it won't hold you back from fully experiencing your life.

This spectrum of experiences connects to both the Brow or Thought Center and the Sacral Center, which is the seat of relationships and pleasure. The acts of both thinking about and feeling the connection with, and subsequent loss of, something or someone loved, produces strong responses from the above centers. Wild thoughts and the total shutdown of desire for pleasure of any kind may commonly occur.

LOSS, EMPTINESS, SADNESS, DEPRESSION

These emotions are natural expressions of the pain of grief, and yet often people are cut short on the time they need to feel these feelings, because of the expectations of others. They are made to feel defective if they can't "get it together" in what others deem a reasonable amount of time. Your sadness is a symptom of your wound and it will only lessen as your wound heals. Emptiness is bound to occur as you adjust to a life without whomever or whatever was lost. You must be patient with yourself, give yourself time to feel and grow through these emotions. Sometimes the full depths of your sadness and emptiness don't hit you until some time has passed. Know that this is normal and surround yourself with compassionate people who will understand, not judge.

Temporary depression is to be expected after experiencing a loss. However, occasionally the feelings of sadness and loneliness become so overwhelming that they will lead to clinical depression. This can be difficult to detect because grief and mourning go hand in hand with many symptoms of depression. It would be wise to seek professional help to work through this kind of depression.

Temporary, fleeting thoughts of suicide can occur while in the depths of sadness and depression. It is natural to experience such thoughts. However, it is ***not natural*** to actually want to take your life. If you have persistent thoughts of taking your life, seek professional help immediately.

This is clearly a Heart Center-based response. Everything is centered on the intense feelings being felt. When the feelings become too overwhelming, the circuits blow out to allow downtime for rest and restoration. This need should really be honored or dangerous repercussions may occur.

RELIEF, RELEASE

This dimension is experienced at the time a loss becomes reality if the experience in the relationship has been one of suffering. This is best exemplified by a death where a long-term illness has occurred and the death brings an end to suffering. However, it is just as applicable in the case of a divorce where the final months of the relationship have been miserable and the divorce brings closure to that ongoing pain. In both these examples, it is important to note that the process of grieving didn't begin at the time the loss actually occurred. It began when the transition of the relationship, from one state to another, began. While we tend to associate the words "relief" and "release" with a positive experience, it doesn't mean that once these emotions are experienced the pain is over. Any of the other dimensions can occur or reoccur after this one. In processing these feelings, it will be important to discuss honestly, the circumstances leading up to the loss, as well as the pain of the loss itself. There is no shame in feeling relief at the end of suffering. That is a normal human response, and as stated before, you have a right and a need to express it.

Although it is perfectly normal and natural to feel relief and release at the end of a long and painful ordeal, we are acculturated to feel that if we are not totally selfless and saintly...we are selfish. That is most certainly not true! There is no "correct" way to grieve.

Of course there are many more manifestations of grief that are possible to experience, and it is important to remember that they can also very well be normal and natural. As long as a given behavior doesn't consume your life, or last an inordinately long time, then it can definitely be part of the huge constellation of emotions that encompass grief.

Remember, grief is a journey not an event. Many feelings and experiences are possible. As they come up, feel them and process them with a safe person. This will keep you moving in a productive, forward manner. You will heal sooner and in a more productive way.

AM I CRAZY?

There are other aspects of the grief journey that are important to become aware of. As with the dimensions of grief, not all of these aspects will be experienced by everyone. However, when experienced, they are destabilizing and frightening enough to often make the griever wonder if he or she is going "crazy." Therefore, I feel it is important to talk about what is possible, so that if it occurs, it will not produce fear and shame.

TIME DISTORTION

It is very common to have difficulty remembering what day or time of day it is. You may not be able to easily pull up what month or year it is. Sometimes there is confusion regarding past and future. As disconcerting as this may be, it is a normal occurrence. A preoccupied mind has difficulty holding onto details. Time distortion is a temporary condition, but can still cause people to feel that they are going crazy.

OBSESSIVE REVIEW OR RUMINATING

Obsessive review is the psychological term for needing to tell your story over and over again. This is an important part of the healing process. Telling the details of the loss over and over helps bring the heart and the head together. During your grief journey, you may need to review the memories of the relationship, as well as the circumstances surrounding the loss, many times. Don't get angry with yourself if you can't seem to stop talking about your loss. It's far healthier to confront and talk about the pain, than it is to try to push it out of your mind. Be easy on yourself, and find safe people who won't mind if you need to tell the story repeatedly.

SEARCH FOR MEANING

We all sometimes need to ask the "Why?" questions. "Why me?" "Why now?" "Why would such a horrible thing happen?" It is normal to try to make sense out of why. There may not be any easy answers, but the questions still burn to be asked. Allow yourself to search for meaning. It is one of the ways we grow spiritually during a grief experience. During this aspect of your grief experience, you may find yourself angry with God or feeling spiritually stagnated. Don't prohibit yourself from feeling the feelings or asking the questions that you need to ask before acceptance can come. One of the best pieces of literature ever written about this period of grief was *A Grief Observed* by C.S. Lewis. It is the publication of the personal journal he kept in the period of time following the death of his beloved wife, Joy. People may try to discourage you from pursuing your search for meaning. Some will try to give you fast, pat answers. You don't have to accept this. If you can find a safe person who will listen and be supportive without the need to provide answers, this can become a time to explore your religious and spiritual values, question your philosophy of life and renew your resources for living.

TRANSITIONAL OBJECTS

These are objects that either belonged to the person lost, or were given to you by them. They are objects invested with meaning and they can be very comforting in the days following a loss. These possessions can help you feel connected to the person who is gone, while you work through the difficult task of accepting the loss. Too many people make the mistake of getting rid of the familiar objects too soon. It is important to embrace the comfort they give you while you need them. When you are ready to let them go, you will know. Some things you may want to keep always. There is nothing wrong with this as long as it doesn't become enshrinement. Enshrinement describes the circumstances when someone keeps everything just as it was long after the loss has occurred. This inability to deal with reality doesn't help the healing. Enshrinement is very different from keeping a few treasured objects, representative of the relationship, which is no longer a part of your life.

GRIEF ATTACKS OR MEMORY EMBRACES

"I thought I was totally over the pain, then I heard that song, and I fell apart." Does this sound familiar? This is a typical description of a grief attack or memory embrace. These are unpredictable episodes when the pain of loss becomes especially acute. They can be totally overwhelming and devastating. They are, however, a very common occurrence. All grieving people have triggers that can be activated by a wide variety of stimuli. Suddenly you may feel an overwhelming sense of missing a person you loved, a place that was special, or a circumstance that has changed. You may instantly and uncontrollably be reduced to tears or some other intense emotion. If this happens to you, don't panic; know that it is normal and be gentle with yourself. The most important thing is to let yourself have the feeling without shame or judgment. Don't try to deny it or stifle it. The energy it takes to do this can really begin to deplete you if it happens often. Also, doing so may eventually lead to emotional, spiritual and physical paralysis.

ANNIVERSARY AND HOLIDAY GRIEF OCCASIONS

These times can produce especially painful grief attacks or memory embraces. These are the times when the presence of someone loved means so very much, and the lack of that presence can be devastating. It is natural to feel particularly lonely or depressed at these times. If you are aware of this possibility, help yourself by planning ahead. Be sure to have support available. Make changes in the ritual if it will torture you to try to do it the same way it was done in the past. Don't be afraid to do what you need to do to take care of yourself. Only you know what you need.

SUDDEN CHANGES IN MOOD

This behavior causes confusion because people wrongly believe that they should follow a pattern of continually feeling better. The truth is, many things can trigger the mood changes that are a normal part of the grief experience. A familiar sight, a song, the wrong things said; any of these things can change a euphoric mood to one of anger, sadness and depression. If you have these ups and downs, be patient with yourself. It will not always be this way, but it can be a confusing, frustrating, lengthy path that must be walked to get to the other side.

IDENTIFICATION SYMPTOMS OF PHYSICAL ILLNESS

This circumstance will most commonly occur when there has been a death, but it can occur with other kinds of losses as well. Sometimes the grieving person will take on symptoms similar to those experienced by a loved one while they were ill. It's a way of identifying and feeling close to the person who is gone. For example, the survivor of someone who died of a brain tumor may start experiencing headaches. It may be chest pains if the death was due to a heart attack. Another case in point would be people who lose someone significant to mental illness, who may start experiencing symptoms similar to the disorder the loved one had. This might be confusion, depression, anxiety, paranoia, or anything else along those lines. If this should happen to you or someone you know, don't be alarmed. Your body is responding to the loss. As you do the work of grieving, these symptoms should dissipate. It would always be advisable, though, to see a doctor and make sure that something more serious isn't causing the problem. Once that is ruled out, then the best course of action is talking to someone you trust about the experience. Journaling can be very beneficial, too.

POWERLESSNESS AND HELPSLESSNESS

Overwhelming feelings of powerlessness and helplessness are a common but debilitating aspect of the grief journey. People often feel powerless over how their grief is manifesting itself. They want to be healing and moving on much faster than they are able to. They may also be very frustrated with the powerlessness they experienced in not having been able to prevent the loss. It is devastating to be forced to deal with a reality you didn't want and didn't choose. Almost paradoxically, by allowing yourself to temporarily experience and process the feelings of helplessness, you are ultimately doing the best you can to help yourself. Trying to be strong can bury feelings, which may eventually manifest themselves in much more troublesome ways.

CRYING AND SOBBING

Tears are the body's means of relieving internal tension, and they allow you to communicate a need to be comforted. *It is much healthier to cry than to repress and deny.* That wouldn't be a bad griever's mantra. Unfortunately, most people get uncomfortable in the presence of a sobbing person. The message not to cry is strongly and frequently delivered, leading to the inevitable repression and denial of feelings for the griever.

Sometimes, early in the grief journey, people experience an inability to cry. This is usually because they are in the dimension encompassing shock and numbness. To experience this temporarily is normal. However, if it becomes long term, help is probably needed. It could be that a buildup of the message not to cry has created a state of chronic numbness. Men are particularly susceptible to this condition because messages like "big boys don't cry" have been denying them their tears since childhood.

Sobbing comes from the inner core of your being. It is an expression of deep, strong emotions within you. Sobbing allows for the release of physical, spiritual and emotional energy. Many other cultures understand this need and encourage sobbing and deep wailing as a normal part of grief. In our culture, sobbing is considered frightening and out of control. The truth, however, is that as you sob, you face the depth of your pain; and this must be done in order to really heal. Tears have a voice of their own, and the wise person allows them the opportunity to speak.

DREAMS

Dreaming about someone you loved who is now lost to you can be very therapeutic. Dreams allow you to feel close to someone who is no longer there. They can be the inner mind's way of coping with the true depth of the pain, or of gently embracing a new reality. Dreams can help you search for meaning or explore unfinished business. They can also give you hope for the future. Talk them over with a safe person who won't be tempted to interpret them. This will be especially important if you are having nightmares. They can be frightening, and discussing them with someone will help diffuse any fear or terror they create, so that they will not precipitate the development of sleep problems.

MYSTICAL EXPERIENCES

The loss of a loved one often creates circumstances that can lead to having a mystical experience. People often report having been visited by the deceased, or feeling an unmistakable presence. Some have experienced an unusual occurrence that felt like a sign that a loved one was all right. In his book, *Understanding Grief,* Dr. Alan Wolfelt tells the story of a mother in Alabama whose daughter had died. She woke up one summer morning, looked out the window and saw it snowing in her yard. The snow lasted fifteen minutes and stopped. She understood this as a communication that her daughter was all right. Others have seen a loved one and been told that all was well. Some have felt an actual embrace of assurance. Unfortunately, most grieving people who share such stories are considered mentally unstable. Yet the stories abound. Most people who have them find them to be very healing. If you have a mystical experience, treasure it and be careful with whom you share it.

LOSS OF INTIMACY AND SEXUALITY

When going through the pain of loss, most people tend to ignore their needs for intimacy and sexuality. They feel too sad or depressed to be physically intimate. It is important to remember that sexual intimacy isn't the only form of intimacy. Being hugged and held or gently touched can be very helpful when you are mourning. This is a basic human need. If your life includes opportunities for this kind of experience, try to give it to yourself. It is possible that the loss you grieve is that of the person with whom you shared physical intimacy. This can make the loss even more difficult to bear. The person you reached out for, who offered you comfort, is now gone. This is another aspect of your life now changed by the loss. Don't deny or minimize the pain this creates. Don't view your sexual needs as inappropriate. Sexuality is normal and can be a powerful force to help reconnect you with life, as long as it is expressed in a healthy way.

DRUGS, ALCOHOL AND GRIEF

Experience suggests that alcohol is the most widely abused self-medication for the bereaved. People are often encouraged by others to have a drink to take the edge off their pain. This is, however, unadvisable. Using alcohol as the vehicle to numb or defocus a person can lead to serious problems. Besides creating psychological dependence on the substance, alcohol abuse inhibits the work of grieving necessary for healing. Too often, sedatives or anti-depressants are prescribed for grieving people, giving them strong messages that their grief isn't okay and that it should be altered. Certainly, there can be circumstances when a temporary, carefully monitored medication may be needed. For the majority of people, however, a more rapid healing results when the work of grieving is done in an unaltered state. There have been far too many instances where long term alcohol and drug abuse has had its origin in avoidance of the pain created by loss.

SELF FOCUS

It is natural to go within when you are in pain. A temporary retreat can feel like the only safe place to be. However, it is important to stress the word "temporary". If this state becomes a life pattern, you are endangering your ability to heal. Healing rarely happens in isolation. There is far too great an emotional overload to handle alone. Talking and writing the pain out is critical to not holding onto it. Some self-focus is needed and appropriate. Don't let anyone push you into reentering life too quickly, but remember the importance of sharing your pain. Not doing so will only stunt or slow down your healing process.

Chapter Three Processes

THE RANT

The purpose of The Rant is to give you the opportunity to release the huge energy of the initial shock. This is where you get to cry out to the heavens how unfair and wrong your loss is. This is where you scream, wail, curse - whatever you feel you need to do, to get this agonizing pain out of your body. This energy is intense and it is real. You need to release it if you are to be able to go forward in a productive way. I know it sucks and the pain is excruciating. It's not fair. Scream that to the heavens, say whatever you need to. This is your time to protest in a powerful way. The method is below.

Have you had a chance to really tell the raw truth to someone about this major change you are experiencing? Have you sat with someone and screamed and cried and cursed the fates that brought this loss upon you? Have you just let it rip, not worrying about the four letter expletives, the way your face looks when you cry, a runny nose or mascara dripping down your anguished cheeks? Have you pounded on pillows, rolled the windows of the car up and screamed while driving down the highway? Have you written about your agony, unleashing it on paper?

If not, you may find that you need to. I'm not saying you have to. There are no have-to-dos in this exercise. Everyone's experience with a major life transition is unique.

It doesn't matter if you lost your home, your dog, your job, your marriage, your trust, your faith in humankind, your money or a dear loved one, you're pissed. This wasn't supposed to happen to you. Even if you knew it was coming, it wasn't supposed to hurt this much. "How can this be? How will I survive? It all feels too huge to deal with!" and truth be told, at the onset of the pain, it *is* too huge to deal with.

At the beginning of your loss, forget social etiquette and appropriate behavior. Instead, Say it like it is. Feel the full magnitude of the pain and shout your protests to the heavens. You have the right to do so. Something just ripped your heart out and you can't sit quietly by.

Do this part in your own way, but I encourage you to go full out in whatever you do. This is no time for soft speech or polite behavior, unless, of course, you are one of those rare people who finds that more comforting. But most of us need to rage a little. Quiet and spiritual solitude often comes in time, but not usually in the moment that your transition begins.

So consider now the time to let it all out. Find a trusted person that you can do this with. Tell them ahead of time that you need to express your outrage and devastation and that you don't know what that will look like. Tell them that you will mostly need them to just sit there quietly, listening supportively, perhaps encouraging you at times or asking an occasional question. But primarily, this time is for you to be present to your pain in the moment, and to express it in any way that feels right to you.

You may need to do this process more than once as different aspects of the loss emerge. However, a word of caution; there's a fine line between authentically expressing your feelings, and becoming them. This is where counseling can be very helpful. We need to feel the feelings and express them fully, but doing that should not become a full time job.

Some of you may find that it is more comfortable to write out what you want to say and to read that out loud in someone else's presence. This part is important. Something special happens when your words are actually heard by other human ears. If you choose to do it this way, try to be as authentic as possible. Be open to leaving your written words and speaking extemporaneously, should the desire to do so strike, or to doing whatever else may come to you in the moment. Sometimes, this is where the most powerful healing takes place.

BREATHING METHODS

Methods such as the ones below serve the purpose of helping you to feel grounded, present, focused and calm. This simple process can also calm and ground you after doing The Rant. It is important to take time to calm down and find balance after that release so that you assist your energy system with normalizing before trying to engage in other activities.

Square Breathing

Square Breathing simply requires you to breathe in to a certain count, and to then hold the breath to the same count. Then breathe out to that count and hold the breath out to the same count before breathing in again. It would look like this:

Breathe in - two, three, four, five, six...

Hold - two, three, four, five, six...

Breathe out - two, three, four, five, six...

Hold - two, three, four, five, six...

Balanced Breathing

When we are stressed and anxious, it is very important that we do everything we can to manage our available energy. Stress is a giant energy drain and we need to take consistent, deliberate action to balance and replenish that energy. The process of balanced breathing is actually derived from an ancient yoga posture.

In studies that have been done on the benefits of this posture, it was found that in cases where a person is in a state of rage so bad as to cause "red out," it normally takes at least twenty minutes to reach homeostasis. However, when doing this posture, that transition time was cut in half. This posture is powerful because you put your body in a position that emulates the infinity sign, which is the way that energy naturally flows. You also create an ongoing energy circuit when you put the tip of your tongue on the roof of your mouth on the "in" breath and then you disconnect it when you put your tongue on the floor of your mouth on the "out" breath. This stop-start motion gets the energy moving and seems to balance Yin and Yang.

This process should be practiced at least twice a day to get the maximum benefit. More often is even better.

To best achieve balanced breathing, start by crossing your left ankle over your right. Extend your arms in front of you and cross your right arm over your left at the wrist. If it is more comfortable for you, this can be reversed with your right ankle over your left and your left arm over your right.

Rotate the palms of your hands so that they are facing and interlock your fingers. Rotate your hands downward and toward your stomach. Then, bring your interlocked hands up to rest against your heart. You have now crossed the center-line of your body with your hands, arms and legs.

Once in position, inhale through the nose while touching the tip of your tongue to the roof of your mouth. Exhale through your lips, resting your tongue on the floor of your mouth. As you breathe, focus on the idea of balance. You might hear the word or visualize something such as a scale, which represents balance to you. Also, focus on feeling calm, centered, grounded, and in a total state of well-being.

Do this for 1 to 3 minutes or more.

Root Center Balancers

The following actions will help to balance this fundamental energy center that is concerned with survival, family values and traditions, connection to the earth, to family and to one's country. These activities energize this energy center, which allows you to feel more grounded, at ease and at peace. This is critical at a time when loss has turned your world upside down.

- Sit on the Earth or walk on it without rubber-soled shoes.
- Visualize the color red swirling at the tip of the spine
- Exercises and Yoga poses that emphasize the legs, knees, and pelvis.
- Aromatherapy using, Cedarwood, Myrrh, Patchouli, Pine, Vetivert, and Ginger.
- Chant "Lahm."
- Wear Gemstones such as Black Onyx, Labradorite, Obsidian, Ruby, Garnet and Hematite.
- Eat red foods like Red Meat or Protein, Root Vegetables, Apples, Red Peppers and Pomegranates.
- Primal, Rhythmic, African or Native American Drumming Music
- Meditation using the Root Center Mudra.
- Massaging the little toe or pinky finger.

EFT – Emotional Freedom Techniques

EFT is probably the most widely known method in the Energy Psychology compendium. It is practiced all over the world because it is a simple and effective way to shift the way you are feeling anytime, anywhere. As we proceed through this book I will be offering suggestions as to what issues you might want to work with at each given phase. However, only you are the expert on you. Feel free to tap on whatever seems to be the present moment preoccupation for you at the time. This is a simple, powerful method that is easily learned and easily practiced on a daily basis. You may find it easier to watch the video that our QR code directs you to so that you can watch me doing it and do it along with me. There are also many videos online of others demonstrating how to do EFT.

Do yourself the favor of learning EFT and using it to assist you with the ups and downs of grieving and in dealing with the changes created by loss.

How It Works

Energy flows through the body. Even though we can't see it, we know it is there by its effects, just like we know that electricity is flowing through a computer because the screen is lit up and the keyboard works.

About 5,000 years ago, the Chinese discovered a complex system of energy circuits that run throughout the body. These energy circuits, or meridians, are the centerpiece of Eastern health practices and form the basis for modern day acupuncture, acupressure and a wide variety of other healing techniques.

The philosophy of EFT, an Energy Psychology method often referred to as Meridian Tapping, developed by Gary Craig in the late 1990's, is that the cause of all negative emotions is a disruption in the body's energy system. By simply tapping near the end points of your energy meridians, you can experience some profound changes in your emotional and physical health. The Gold Standard EFT Tutorial explains it this way:

> *"EFT breathes fresh air into the healing process by borrowing from the Chinese meridian system. While acupuncture, acupressure and the like have been primarily focused on physical ailments, EFT stands back from this ancient process and points it also at emotional issues. These, in turn, often provide benefits for performance and physical issues.*
>
> *EFT combines the physical benefits of acupuncture with the cognitive benefits of conventional therapy for a much faster, more complete treatment of emotional issues, and the physical and performance issues that often result.*
>
> ### *EFT is an emotional version of acupuncture, except we don't use needles.*
>
> *While related to acupuncture, EFT does not use needles. Instead, we use a simple two-pronged process wherein we (1) mentally "tune in" to specific issues while (2) stimulating certain meridian points on the body by tapping on them with our fingertips. Properly done, EFT appears to balance disturbances in the meridian system and thus often reduces the conventional therapy procedures from months or years down to minutes or hours. The basic Tapping process is easy to learn, can be done anywhere, and can be used to provide impressive do-it-yourself results."*

http://www.emofree.com/eft-tutorial/tapping-basics/what-is-eft.html A chart of these meridian points will follow.

The procedure consists of the participant rating the emotional intensity of their reaction to an emotionally distressing situation on a **Subjective Units of Distress Scale** (SUDS). This is a **Likert scale** for subjective measures of distress, calibrated from 0 -10. No emotional distress would be a 0 and a 10 would be extreme emotional distress.

The participant then repeats an orienting **affirmation statement** (e.g. "Feeling distressed and anxious.") while rubbing or tapping specific points on the body. After tapping, the emotional intensity is rescored and the tapping repeated until the SUDS score is a 0.

The combination of tapping the energy meridians while focusing on the problem calms or neutralizes the energy disruption. It clears the short-circuit (or emotional block) from your body's bioenergy system, thus restoring your mind and body's balance, which is essential for optimal health and healing.

It is important to note that EFT has basic approaches that can be applied by anyone, as well as more in depth professional uses. I highly recommend that if you seek a professional to assist you with using EFT, you find one who has been well trained.

The suggestions I include are for doing a very basic form of EFT to gain some relief from the intense emotional feelings created by the loss. This is so you can attain a level of calm that will enable you to participate in life and eventually do other work.

While Official EFT doesn't recommend using scripts, because the general nature of them can't address the specific issues of each individual, I include them to give you examples of some of the kinds of things you might want to tap on. While these are some suggestions that might get you started to get the most out of EFT, you would want to clear the intensity from the specific events that happened to you either with a professional or by studying parts 1 and 2 of the EFT

Tutorial, using the Personal Peace Procedure. (http://www.emofree.com/eft-tutorial/tapping-basics/how-to-do-eft.html)

Below is a chart of the points we tap in doing EFT or Meridian Tapping.

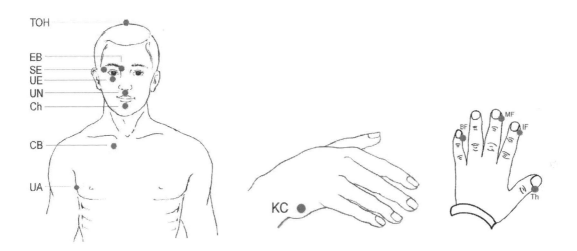

Possible Steps and Scripts for using EFT in Phase One

1. After determining the distress level (SUDS), while tapping the Karate Chop Point you should say:

   "Even though I am shocked, devastated and out of control, I deeply and completely accept myself." We speak a negative statement to highlight the condition that we want corrected. Much like highlighting on your computer the statement that you want to delete. Then go on to tap each of the points repeating the statement. Feel free to augment the statement to better describe specifically what you are feeling.

2. Tapping the Top of the Head: "Shocked, devastated and out of control."

3. Tapping the Inner Eyebrow: "Shocked, devastated and out of control."

4. Tapping the Side of the Eye: "Shocked, devastated and out of control."

5. Tapping Under the Eye: "Shocked, devastated and out of control."

6. Tapping Under the Nose: "Shocked, devastated and out of control."

7. Tapping Under the Lip: "Shocked, devastated and out of control."

8. Tapping Under the Collarbone: "Shocked, devastated and out of control."

9. Tapping Under the Arm: "Shocked, devastated and out of control."

10. If you choose, go on to tapping the finger points, making the same statement. Sometimes they are very helpful, especially when dealing with physical symptoms such as tightness in the chest from anxiety. In many instances, you can skip them and just repeat the treatment starting back on the top of the head.

11. After completing the treatment segment check your SUDS to see if the number has reduced. Keep repeating the tapping until you feel that you have reached a 0. If a new aspect of your emotional reaction comes to you, like realizing that your feelings of shock, devastation and being out of control are really aspects of your terror of what the future holds, then switch to tapping on "Terrified about what the future holds."

12. Once 0 or Neutral has been reached, although it is not part of Official EFT, I like to insert a positive statement. In this case, for example, we might start tapping at the Top of the Head saying: "I am calm, accepting and in a state of faith and trust." Something that describes how you want to feel. Tap this positive statement into each point for 3 rounds then see if you are resonating with it.

Journaling

Journaling

Journaling

_____

_____

_____

_____

_____

_____

_____

_____

_____

_____

_____

_____

_____

_____

_____

_____

_____

_____

_____

_____

_____

_____

_____

_____

CHAPTER FOUR

I Get By with a Little Help from My Friends

"Do you need anybody? I need somebody to love."

The Beatles (*With a Little Help from My Friends*)

The Energy: Connected, Seeking Support, Interactive – Relating to the Sacral Energy Center or Chakra.

The Action: Talk to trusted friends, professionals, support groups and loved ones

Once emotional pain and grief has you in its grip, only action gets you out. After we stop screaming, blaming bad luck or fate, and over-focusing on the details that caused the loss, it's time to turn around and begin our journey through the mire of this unexpected, unwelcomed set of circumstances.

The energy is heavy and deadening; it needs to be shifted and lightened. We can do this best by engaging in daily activities that get our energy moving. It is also important to interact with, and talk to, "safe" people. Helpful, important behaviors at this point in the journey might include attending grief support groups, using Energy Psychology and other mind/body processes, going to professional counseling, journaling, looking for meaning in the loss, avoiding isolation, being as authentic as possible, and being easy on yourself.

We need to remember that there is no "correct" way to grieve. Wherever we are, whatever we are feeling, and whatever we are doing, is okay. As we said, there are no *Five Stages of Grief,* and there is no set timeline for grieving, it is all normal.

Connection with trusted, supportive friends, family and professionals is critical at this time. It is often impossible to understand why a given loss has happened. We can privately agonize over the "whys" or we can wrestle with them verbally with others who are good listeners, others who don't feel the need to fix us but can allow us to talk, feel, and emote as much as we need to.

This is a great time to join a good grief support group whose goal is to help you move through your loss, rather than sitting in it, ruminating interminably. We need to express our feelings but not become them.

A word of caution seems appropriate here: Some grief groups do more to perpetuate sadness and victim mentality than they do to help people heal. They don't have a planned progression. They just provide a weekly format for people to indulge in sadness and victim mentality. I don't feel this is advantageous. A grief group should be supporting movement toward re-entering life and vibrant living. It is important to be engaged in some kind of group that supports you and encourages your growth, not one that enables and encourages you to stay stuck.

In the last step we looked at the normal, natural freak-out that happens when a loss or life transition first occurs. We talked about the cry of anguish that goes up when a crippling loss creates the impossible circumstances that we now must endure. But after that upheaval subsides, and the relentless obsession with the circumstances that created the loss begins to quiet its ever-present voice; it's time to absorb the reality of the loss and begin to contemplate how to move forward and recover from the devastation.

For some, this will happen more quickly and easily. Others writhe in the agony of loss for years. There is no one size fits all mentality in dealing with life transitions. Each person's journey is unique to them and to their loss. It may not be a long painful stay; it may only involve a few days of introspection. Sometimes it's only the length of a good cleansing cry. But too often, the stay is unpredictable, intimidating, emotional and fraught with fear and loneliness.

The processes I will share with you can certainly make this time shorter and more productive. They will also give you a sense of power within circumstances that can so easily make you feel powerless.

The Sacral Energy Center

During this aspect of the experience of dealing with loss, we are focused in the body's Sacral Center or Chakra. This center is about connection and relationships, support from others, pleasure and creativity. It is important to be interacting with supportive friends and family. We can actually gain energy and shift the heaviness of our energy by interacting with loving, supportive, vibrant, funny, understanding people.

Engaging in creative pursuits that aren't stress inducing can be very therapeutic. A perfect example of this would be the beautiful memory-book a friend created after losing her infant son. It contained all sorts of things: cards, his birth certificate, ultrasound pictures, bits of clothing, the shower invitation and pictures of everything that had been a memorable part of his short life. It is still something she treasures.

Giving ourselves nurturing moments of pleasure can be very helpful. Hot, scented baths, relaxing naps, walks in lovely gardens or naturally beautiful places can soothe and calm us during this turbulent time. Quiet contemplation, comfortable clothing, lovely fragrances, and warm, nutritious comforting foods all serve us well while we are in this vulnerable state.

It is hard to get through this difficult time alone. Support from at least one loving person is critical. Expressing the feelings and talking to a non-judgmental, supportive listener helps us to move through them. Without that, we can become trapped in our own, fearful, negative ideas about the situation. Being around others who understand our pain can act as a jump-start to our tired worn out batteries.

Read:

The Power of Intention (pg. 83), 20 Things to Say and Not to Say to People in Pain (pg. 86)

Processes:

Complete the writing of your Intention Statement, Practice *Balanced Breathing* (pg. 94) several times a day. Do the Global PR Correction and The Occipital Hold every day (pg. 95) Sacral Center Balancers (pg. 96) EFT (pg. 97) Find safe people to process your pain with.

GPRC   Occipital Hold

EFT

Journal:

Journal about what has happened and how it impacts your hopes for the future. How do you feel about talking about the loss, change, or transition? What kind of people or settings are ones you could be comfortable with? What do you need to be different in order to begin to feel some possibility of ever feeling joyful and alive again? You may also want to write about what you learned in the piece on 20 Things to Say and Not To Say and how this will affect your communication with people in pain and with people trying to help you with your pain. And of course, feel free to write about anything else that is important to you at this time.

THE POWER OF INTENTION

Intention is a powerful way of harnessing energy and heading it in the direction you want it to go. And as we now know from the teachings of Quantum Physics, everything is made of energy, vibrating at different frequencies.

Energy is random, kind of like a room full of ping-pong balls bouncing and shooting around in every direction. When we set an intention, it's as if a large suction tube scoops the ping-pong balls up and shoots them out the other end in a direction that we desire them to go. I think of it as being similar to the workings of a laser beam. Somehow, through a technology that is way over my head, a laser device gathers the energy, shoots it through a crystal and turns it into a powerful beam of light that can do many amazing things. In this form, energy is far more useful than a bunch of random atoms, photons and bosons shooting about in every direction. This is the function of Intention; it focuses those powerful bits of energy so they can be utilized for creating something wonderful.

With this in mind, you can hopefully see how valuable it would be to set an intention regarding the healing that you would like to have take place in your life. Having a stated intention creates a goal, a target to shoot for. This is made even more powerful by putting it in writing.

This point is well illustrated in the following study. According to this Harvard Business School study, written goals can translate into earnings of 10 times more than those who fail to establish goals or put their goals in writing. In this study, Harvard graduates were asked if they had goals and, if so, whether or not those goals were written down. Only 3% had written their goals down, 11% had goals but had not written them down and 86% had not yet established goals.

Twenty years later, the same group was polled. The 11% who had goals but had not written them down were making twice as much as the 86% who had no goals. However, the 3% who had written down their goals were making over 10 times more than the average of all the other graduates, and 98% of all the wealth resided within that same 3%! *(Harvard Business School study, 1987 and 2007)*

The Process

On a separate sheet of paper, please write a paragraph or more, describing how you will look and feel when you have reconciled your present loss issues and reached the state of healing that you desire. Put as much detail into the description as possible. Here are some areas to consider:

· How will you feel upon waking in the morning and where will you be?

· What will your energy level be like?

· What will you do for work and for fun?

· How will you feel about the relationships in your life?

· How do you want to feel regarding the relationship you are working on?

· What areas of your life and what challenges are you better able to handle?

· How will your body look and feel?

· What will a typical day in your life look like?

The Reason

You might be wondering why we are doing this. The answer is simple and yet incredibly powerful. If we aren't clear about our intention, how will we ever achieve our goals? If you decide to take a journey but you don't know where you're going, how will you ever know when you've arrived? If we don't have a picture of what success looks like, how will we know when we have succeeded?

So often in life, we pray for our dreams to come true but we don't really have a clear vision of that dream. How then can we expect this cloudy abstraction to become our dream life? We need to empower our hopes and dreams with as much shape and clarity as possible.

Write your intention out in detail, read it everyday, visualize it, feel it, stay positive, and look out... because you're going to create it!

20 Things to Say, and Not to Say to People in Pain

Over the years of counseling grieving people, I have been asked a hundred times, "What do I say to someone who has just lost a child or a husband or a job? I'm afraid to call, because I don't know what to say or how to help."

Have you been there? I think we all have at one time or another. Because this dilemma is so common, I wrote the following piece to give a concrete answer to people who are genuinely intimidated by the prospect of being in the presence of someone who has just suffered profound grief and loss. I don't know about you, but they didn't offer Grief 101 at my school. So how are we supposed to know how to be truly helpful and not patronizing or even abusive?

Listen.

People in pain need to be listened to, not supplied with answers. They know deep inside that there are no explanations to the most important questions they are asking themselves, and they aren't really expecting answers from those who console them. If we truly wish to respond to the needs of those who are grieving, our consoling actions should typically begin with a distinct emphasis on listening, not talking. There is power in the silence of listening, and a clear message: "I'm right here, I care and I'm with you. I may not be sure what to say, but I'm ready to listen."

Real listening comes from the heart, where sympathy and healing begin. To listen intently, the listener must be fully present in the moment. It requires practice and energy, but the effect can be amazing. When the listener puts all other thoughts aside and truly listens empathically, the speaker's emotional floodgates may open and release long pent-up feelings. As this deep listening continues, the speaker often comes up with his or her own solutions to problems. This is a tremendous gift to give to someone in pain.

Listen without judgment and respond with *feeling* words. ("How painful." "What frustration!" "Sounds so heartbreaking." How devastating." "What confusion this must create for you." "It's so sad." "How lonely.")

Being a good listener is difficult if your own issues of loss are unresolved. Discomfort or anxiety might arise and take you out of the moment if the speaker's conversation touches upon issues that still cause you pain. In the best-case scenario, your own grief work would be completed and these unresolved issues wouldn't exist. However, if this should not be the case, the best course of action would be to tell the speaker honestly what you are feeling, and then try to get back to discussion of his/her situation.

Once you have taken time to listen, healing conversation can begin. Remember grief is emotional, not intellectual! Helpful conversations need to encourage emotional outlet. Here are some helpful remarks with which you might start:

HELPFUL THINGS TO SAY:

1. "What happened?"

2. "I'm so sorry. Was he/she ill for a long time?"

3. "I've been thinking about you and wanted to know how you were doing."

4. "This must be a bewildering and incredibly complicated time."

5. "What's it like for you these days? How are you coping?"

6. "I can't imagine how painful this must be."

7. "Were you able to have any meaningful conversations with him/her before the end?"

8. "Do you feel like talking for awhile?"

9. "When did you first realize the seriousness of the situation?"

10. "I certainly can't know exactly how your pain feels, but I remember when I lost my Mom...." (Remember: share don't compare.)

11. "This can be such a lonely time. How is it going for you?"

12. "You know one of my favorite memories of him was..."

13. "Each person's grief process is unique. What kinds of things are you experiencing?"

14. "There is so much going on for you right now and it can be so overwhelming. Want to talk about it?"

15. "I have never experienced anything exactly like this but I remember the time...(share how you felt to help open up the griever.)

16. "Don't worry, I'm not going to tell you that everything happens for a reason. Right now I'm sure you just feel that this sucks."

17. "Just so you know I am totally on board for helping you in any way that I can: driving you somewhere, bringing you food...whatever."

18. "I'm sorry that I didn't call sooner. Quite honestly I didn't know what to say."

19. "Whether you feel like talking or not I am here and I'm not going anywhere."

20. "I wish I knew the perfect thing to say to make it better but I don't. I do love you though."

THE FOLLOWING ARE NOT HELPFUL:

1. "You must get on with your life; you've been grieving long enough."

2. "I know it's tough, but you're not the first person this has happened to."

3. "Be thankful you have another child."

4. "Don't cry; tears wont help anything."

5. "I know exactly what you're going through."

6. "We have no right to question God's will."

7. "You're young; you have plenty of time to find another relationship."

8. "It was really a blessing; you mustn't be selfish."

9. "You're lucky you had him for so long."

10. "Don't feel guilty or ashamed; you're only human."

11. "You must hold yourself together for the sake of the children."

12. "I heard you're not taking it too well."

13. "You know grief just takes time."

14. "You've got to keep yourself busy so you don't think about it."

15. "It could have been worse."

16. "It's for the best; you deserve a better relationship."

17. "God never gives a burden bigger than the back can bear. You'll be fine."

18. "I'm sorry but we all have to go sometime."

19. "It's just a house (or a job or a pet or a...) there will be another one."

20. "You have to know that God knows best, there's a reason for everything. You're going to grow through this."

While some of the above statements may be intellectually accurate, they are ineffective and possibly even abusive. Grief is an emotional state, not an intellectual one! The head isn't broken; the heart is. Emotion is the medicine of the heart. People in emotional states only feel HEARD if they are responded to with emotion. People in pain need to relate to our humanity, not our database!

Remember the most important ingredient in helping someone in pain is the intention of your heart. Stay present and stay in your intention to comfort and support. If you do this, you will know the right things to say.

If any part of you thinks you need to get the griever to "snap out of it and move on," please don't act on it, give them their space. None of us has the right to say "time's up" in regards to someone else's pain. Believe me, no one wants to be hurting any longer than they have to, but they also can't be what they are not.

Let me make this as simple and clear as I can:

Be present

Have the intention to comfort and support without judgment

Listen

Respond from the heart

Allow the person who is hurting whatever time and process they need.

Sometimes if you are the person in pain it can be equally hard to know how to tell others what you need and what you want. Often the one who is agonizing is worrying about being a *downer* to others and consequently, don't get their true needs met and the pain keeps growing. This often leads to isolation, which is not conducive to healing.

Here are some suggestions of ways to communicate to others how you feel and what you need.

WHAT TO SAY IF YOU ARE THE PERSON IN PAIN:

1. "Thank you for your concern, it means a great deal to me but I just need to be alone right now."

2. "I am really having a hard time talking but could you just sit with me without talking?"

3. "What I really need is a hug."

4. "There really is nothing to say. It is what it is but I appreciate your being here."

5. "Maybe God needed him but I need him too and it isn't comforting to hear that right now."

6. "There really don't seem to be any good answers. I'm just trying to get through one moment at a time."

7. "Quite honestly the future looks terrifying, empty and grim. I don't know what to do."

8. "I don't expect you to say the perfect words it just feels good that you're here."

9. "I want to be alone and yet I don't. Could you come and just watch a movie with me?"

10. "Just taking a walk in silence would be so helpful. Would you do that with me?"

11. "I appreciate your suggestions and when I have a little more energy I will try them."

12. "It's so hard to keep up the façade, thank you for allowing me to be real."

13. "I don't know what I need but it feels good that you care and are trying."

14. "Everyone has answers and suggestions and I appreciate the efforts that are being made but I am clear that I am going to have to find those answers for myself."

15. "If you would like to bring by some food, that would be great but I need to warn you that I am not very good company right now."

16. "I just need to feel what I'm feeling until I'm not feeling it anymore. Hopefully you understand."

17. "I hear what you're saying but have you ever experienced anything like this?"

18. "Just to know that you're there when I'm ready to talk is a blessing."

19. "I need time to cry and feel the pain and I'm just not ready to socialize just yet."

20. "Your love is a blessing that feels like a life raft in a sea of pain. Thank you for being there."

Chapter Four Processes

GPRC

(Global Psychoenergetic Reversal Correction)

This process is calming, affirming and helps one come to a greater state of self-love and acceptance. It is especially effective to do while standing in front of a mirror looking into (not at) your own eyes.

Rubbing the NLR (Neurolymphatic reflex) spots on the upper chest a few inches below the collarbones, in an outward direction, say the following three times:

"I deeply and completely love and accept myself with all my problems, challenges and strengths."

The Occipital Hold

When going through the emotional roller coaster of grief it is so easy to have your head going in a million different directions. You may even feel that parts of you are scattered all over the planet. This process will help you to feel grounded, whole, in your body and able to think more clearly.

Place one hand across the forehead with fingers pointing toward the ear and the other hand at the base of the skull with fingers pointing toward the other ear. This creates transformative electrical contact between the meridians in your hands and the acu-points on your head.

Breathe deeply and evenly, concentrating on feeling centered, focused and whole. Call back any parts of you that are scattered out there in the Universe at your place of work, with your love interest, with your children, family members or any places or situations that are preoccupying your attention. Bring everything to your center and feel a sense of wholeness and power. Feel yourself grounded in your body. Do this for a few minutes, or as long as feels good.

Sacral Center Balancers

These activities help to balance and energize this energy center that is concerned with relationships with others, creativity and pleasure. It is a very important center for those dealing with the upheaval of loss because we have to be able to reach out to others for help, we need creative ideas and solutions to figure out how to deal with our circumstances and we must be able to give ourselves moments of nurturing and enjoyment.

- Floating in water
- Visualizing Orange in the abdominal region
- Exercises and Yoga poses that focus on the abdomen and low back
- Aromatherapy with Bergamot, Rose, Sandalwood or Musk
- Chanting "Vahm"
- Wearing gemstones like Carnelian, Citrine, Golden Topaz, Coral or Rose Quartz
- Eating orange foods like Persimmons, Oranges, Orange Peppers, Carrots, Tangerines and Salmon
- Listening to flowing, New Age music, Chopin or Brahms
- Meditating with hands in Sacral Center Mudra
- Massaging the fourth toe or ring finger.

EFT Tapping Suggestions

Again, after determining what your SUDS is on a specific issue, tap on all the points shown in the chart in Chapter Two (pg. 71) As examples of the kinds of things you would tap on in this phase, here are some statements:

1. "Even though everyone is into their lives and I feel so alone, I deeply and completely accept myself." Then tap all the points saying, "In pain and alone."

2. "Even though no one seems to understand and it makes me angry, I..." Then tap all the points saying, "No one gets it and I'm angry."

3. "Even though I ache all the time, I...." Then tap all the points saying, "Aching all the time."

4. "Even though my partner can't relate and I feel so alone...." Then tapping all the points say, "My partner can't relate and I feel so alone."

5. "Even though I want to be held but I don't want to be with anybody, I...." Tapping all of the points, say "Want to be held but want to be alone."

After doing several rounds assess your SUDS and repeat the statement, or adjust it to be more specific to what you are currently feeling.

When you feel you have reached a 0, think of a positive condition you would like to be experiencing and tap that into all of the points in 3 rounds. Here is an example: "I am open and honest with safe people," or "I sleep soundly and peacefully and my body is comfortable at all times."

Journaling

Journaling

Journaling

_____

_____

_____

_____

_____

_____

_____

_____

_____

_____

_____

_____

_____

_____

_____

_____

_____

_____

_____

_____

_____

_____

_____

_____

_____

CHAPTER FIVE

Let It Be

"There will be an answer, let it be."

The Beatles (*Let it Be*)

The Energy: Self-Focused, Self-Caring, and Introspective – Relating to the Solar Plexus Center or Chakra.

The Action: Take care of yourself and engage in activities that are healing and nurturing. Create rhythm and consistency in your daily life. Pay attention to your thoughts, feelings, nutrition, sleep, exercise and activities.

At this point, your energy is stronger and more stable but it needs to be recharged, amplified and supported in order to help prepare you to live in a new normal. What is really beneficial now is daily engagement in healthy, life enhancing activities. This could include meditation and prayer, exercise, gratitude processes, actively challenging your mind to prioritize positive thinking, watching uplifting movies and reading life-enhancing materials that light up your heart and soul.

Your grief experience is your own and you must do it your own way. Remember that whatever we focus on, we feed energy to, and whatever we feed energy to, grows. Try to focus on positive, life-enhancing thoughts. Avoid dwelling on negative, energy depleting thoughts. Keep choosing the thought that feels better and soon you will feel better.

This is a time of introspection and personal growth - a time to find meaning in the life transition or loss that you have experienced. You might find comfort in creating certain daily rituals, like lighting a candle every morning and blessing yourself, saying a certain prayer, reading a passage from a meaningful book, or doing yoga.

The first thing that is important to know is that you have *Rights* as a person going through emotional pain and upheaval. You don't have to be polite and sit quietly by as *well meaning* people say thoughtless things that hurt you. Be informed and pro-active. Even when the intention is to help you, most people are very inept at knowing what to say. There is no Grief 101, so when we come up against a situation where someone we love is going through a tough life transition, we utter inane, unhelpful, and often, untrue things like:

"I guess God needed him more than you did."

"Just keep busy to take your mind off the pain."

"You just have to give it time. Time heals all wounds."

Don't be afraid to speak up and say, "I know you are trying to be helpful, but right now I just need to feel my feelings and not look for answers, because nothing is making any sense."

Or you can keep it simple and just say, "Thank You," before walking away. Bottom line, do whatever you need to do to take care of yourself. You are in a fragile, emotional state and you need some loving care. Don't be afraid to give it to yourself. No one knows better than you, what you need.

Unfortunately, most of us aren't very good at nurturing ourselves. We excel at criticizing, chastising and exhausting ourselves, but we aren't very good at loving, honoring and caring tenderly for ourselves. Please make an effort to improve your skills in this area. Your healing depends on it. Take care of yourself like you would take care of your child or anyone else that was special to you. You are hurting and you deserve all the TLC you can get.

Solar Plexus Center

This phase of the journey through loss really centers on you, and that is what the energy of the Solar Plexus Energy Center is all about. Self-concepts, self-criticism, the ego and personality all reside in this center. If we are not careful, we can enter into a lot of self-criticism during this time. It is so easy to feel defective because we can't find a way to feel better, and it seems that everyone else can figure it out except us. We might also become oversensitive to other's opinions and exceptionally needy about having control. This is due to the fact that the world seems out of control, so we want to hold on in any way we can.

The most important thing to do at this time is to turn your focus to the self; love and nurture yourself. Get off your own back and allow yourself to feel badly about how things have gone.

Know that it won't always be like this, but that the key is to be present. Feel it and allow it in so that it can then pass through.

That is how the emotional system is designed to work. The problems get created when we don't do this. When instead, we try to carry nobly on and do everything we normally would. In order to pull this off, we have to stuff the emotional pain somewhere, which then creates a block in the flow of our energy. These blocks become what author Michael Singer (*The Untethered Soul*) has called "our cherished wounds." We end up tending these wounds and living around them as if we had a thorn in our sides that we were trying to avoid people bumping into. We limit ourselves, and our activities in order to protect ourselves from feeling the pain of the thorn being bumped.

We can't project ourselves fully into the world if we are engaged in this type of living. Life becomes all about caution and limitation, which is not living out loud. Don't let yourself fall down that tunnel. Take the risk, feel the pain and express it so that you can move through it and not tuck it away to haunt you another day.

Read:

Read "Why Myths, Misinformation and Intellectual Concepts Don't Help " (pg. 108).

Then read "The Life Transitions Bill of Rights" (pg. 113) and express what you are going through honestly to at least two people, or to your grief group.

Processes to Do:

The Pain and the Payoff, (pg. 117) The Head and Heart Breath several times each day (pg. 119) When you feel ready, add Donna Eden's Emotional Overload Calming Procedure. (pg.

120) Consider committing to a daily meditation practice or some kind of ritual that gives you a moment of introspection and appreciation. Join a group that promotes getting outside and moving your body. If this doesn't appeal to you, go for daily walks or hikes alone and soak in the beauty around you, or practice self-reflection. Rhythm and routine are very important now and combining that with something that enhances you spiritually and emotionally is particularly beneficial.

It will also be very helpful to engage in the Solar Plexus Balancers (pg. 123) and EFT (pg. 125)

Head & Heart Breath   Separating Heaven & Earth

EFT

Journal:

How family patterns and societal teachings have affected your ability to experience loss and life transitions. Journal about the practices or habits you are developing that embody self-care. Identify the "Rights," from the *Bill of Rights* piece, that really speak to you and how you will procure them for yourself. Always feel free to journal about whatever moves you, let your heart have unlimited time to speak.

WHY MYTHS, MISINFORMATION AND INTELLECTUAL CONCEPTS DON'T HELP

MYTHS and MISINFORMATION are incorrect ideas about how to deal with loss, mistaken ideas which have usually been handed down from generation to generation. Unfortunately, they have little value in actually helping anyone heal from the pain of loss. In fact, they are detrimental because people believe they are valid, so they try to do whatever the myths might suggest they do. When no healing or easing of the pain results, the people involved often feel that something is wrong with them.

"This seems to work for everybody else but not for me. What's the matter with me?"

This fear and frustration only complicates the already painful experience. The truth is that nothing is wrong with the person in pain. Their responses are perfectly normal. The problem is with the faulty information they have been given. Some examples of Myths and Misinformation are:

"Grief just takes time."

"Talking about your pain just makes it worse."

"Keeping busy is the best thing to do after experiencing a significant emotional loss."

INTELLECTUAL CONCEPTS are the things people say that may be intellectually accurate, but that are of no value in helping someone who is dealing with an emotional issue.

These types of statements are usually borne out of the discomfort of the speaker, who probably wants to be helpful but doesn't know how to do so effectively. The majority of people have no training in how to best help an emotional person, so they fall back on what they are most comfortable with... intellect. Rather than listening to the person's pain and responding with emotional words and understanding, they feel compelled to come up with solutions and try to fix the griever. They advise, criticize and judge, though they may not ever mean to do so. They feel they've succeeded if they get the person in pain to stop emoting. When in fact, the opposite is often true.

One of the reasons that intellectual concepts are so ineffective in emotional situations is that the griever's head is not broken, his heart is. In short, an emotional situation is best helped by an emotional, or feeling based, response such as:

"How terrifying!"

"That must have been devastating for you."

"How awful, I'm so sorry."

These kinds of responses are much more helpful than statements like:

"It was just God's will."

"You're better off without him."

"At least she won't have to suffer now."

"You've just got to go forward, life must go on."

Here are some of the most common Myths and Misinformation:

A. **Time heals all wounds.**

I'm going to make this real simple. Time, alone, doesn't heal anything. It's what we do with the time that can make a difference.

So... the question to ask is, "What am I willing to do? What am I willing to try, in order to get out of emotional pain and feel alive again?"

B. **There are predictable stages of grief.**

This is one of my pet peeves. There are no predictable stages of grief. There are common experiences and some phases that seem to be universal, but on the whole, grief is an experience that is unique to everyone.

The origin of this myth is Elizabeth Kubler Ross's work on *Death and Dying*.

She identified stages of Death and Dying and people have been mistakenly calling them the Stages of Grief for years. Again, people mean well, they are just passing on the misinformation that they have learned from others.

I have had way too many people come to me totally distraught because they fear that they are not *grieving right* because they didn't experience all of the *stages.* Therefore, I feel very strongly about trying to correct this damaging piece of misinformation.

C. **It is best to get busy and move away from grieving.**

This one is confusing because it has a shred of truth. We do need to allow ourselves to experience and express the pain and tears that grief creates. Especially in the beginning, it is almost impossible to do anything but cry and agonize in pain. This is normal and needs to happen. I encourage you to do this.

Yet, at the same time, I caution you not to allow prolonged emotional extremes that result in retreating from the world or going into a fetal ball and sobbing all day long.

It's critical to find a balance point between expressing painful feelings and becoming them. We need the opportunity to experience our heartbreak, but this must be balanced with staying involved in our lives and our responsibilities.

D. **When dealing with a grieving person, try to cheer them up. Don't bring up the loss and make them feel bad.**

This idiocy is practiced by nearly everyone in our culture. I ask you, when you have just experienced a significant loss, is there any moment in time when you aren't acutely aware of it?

It is difficult enough to put it toward the back of your mind so you can try to function, but to have to pretend everything's fine on top of that just makes everything more difficult. The only thing we do when we don't bring up the loss is put pressure on the griever to put on a game face and engage in the charade with us. It is much better to be honest and up front, even if all you can say is "I don't know what to say."

The best thing we can do is to acknowledge the loss and get it out in the open. Say something like, "I feel so bad about your loss. I can't imagine how painful this must be."

Then shut up and let the griever talk. That's helpful and just might actually cheer them up eventually, because truth has a way of doing that.

THE LIFE TRANSITIONS BILL OF RIGHTS

The Original Concept of Alan Wolfelt

- **You have the right to acknowledge your reality and experience your pain in your own unique way.**

Don't let others tell you how to grieve or put you on any type of a timetable. The same goes for the so-called Stages of Grief. There are no set stages that everyone does or should go through to heal "properly." Each encounter with loss is unique, period.

- **You have the right to talk about your pain, and to be listened to, without advice or opinion.**

You have the right to be able to express your feelings and your pain through talking about them. This can be very healing, but be sure to find others who can listen without judgment or opinion. You need to be heard far more than you need to be advised. Also, remember that if you don't want to talk, that choice should be honored as well. Find people who will just be with you in silence

- **You have the right to feel and express a huge constellation of emotions.**

Loss can be a roller coaster ride of emotions. There is no rhyme or reason as to how those emotions come or when. You need to be patient with yourself and allow what is normal and natural to happen. Try to allow the feelings and experience them. Talk them over, journal about them, cry them out, find an art media through which to express them, whatever works for you. The old saying, "better out than in," applies completely when it comes to emotions.

- **You have the right to pace yourself physically and emotionally, and to honor your limits.**

Experiencing loss is a lot like being hit by a Mac Truck. You are wounded, emotionally bleeding, and there is extreme pain from a broken heart. If you were hit by a truck and in a body cast, you would be easy on yourself and would respect your limitations. Do the same for yourself after being hit by the Mac Truck called LOSS. Get plenty of rest, eat well and don't push yourself beyond what you are ready for.

- **You have the right to experience unexpected waves of grief, ranging from small and manageable, to tsunamis.**

This journey through loss has many unexpected turns. It has no set progression or stages. It happens in a huge variety of unexpected ways. It comes in waves of all states and sizes, seemingly at its own will. Strange as it may sound, the unpredictability of the emotions of loss is the one thing you can count on.

- **You have the right to embrace your Spirituality. And through it, to seek comfort and meaning in your loss.**

Spiritual beliefs and practices can be very helpful in healing. Finding a sense of meaning in what you are going through is often essential to accepting the loss. Sometimes grief produces anger at God or a challenge to one's faith. If this is your experience, know that you are not alone. Process these feelings with someone safe that can listen without judgment.

- **You have the right to use Ritual to support and comfort you.**

It can be helpful and comforting to have certain rituals that you practice as you navigate loss. Saying prayers, lighting candles, or anything else you have found comforting in the past can help you feel connected to what you have lost and can help ease the transition you are going through.

- **You have the right to process the experiences of the relationship accurately to assist you in grieving the reality of what was, rather than the euphoric recall of it.**

It is impossible to reconcile or complete the loss of a villain or a saint. All relationships have positive and negative aspects. It is best to remember the relationship in a balanced way so that you don't get stuck in a spiral of bitterness toward a villain, or endless devotion to a saint. These spirals keep you stuck in a kind of grief loop that prevents healing and moving forward.

- **You have the right to talk about and cherish your memories.**

Your memories are precious and important, a great source of comfort. They are the treasures that you have left, the connection with what you have lost. Don't cut yourself short by not talking about them out of fear that you will cry or upset others. Give yourself the gift of cherishing and talking about your memories.

- **You have the right to utilize effective tools and procedures to help you move to a place of acceptance, healing and the ability to move beyond loss, to growth and transformation.**

Grief doesn't have to be a life sentence, but time alone doesn't heal the wounds. Taking action to process and heal your pain is what creates effective results. We are far more powerful than we realize. If we are willing to step into that power and do what we must to reconcile the grief, we can emerge with depth and wisdom, as well as a renewed appreciation of life and joy.

THE PAIN AND THE PAYOFF

When life seems hopeless and overwhelming and you can't see any light at the end of the tunnel, doing this process can revive your hope that light and joy may one day be possible.

Life is unpredictable. It can seem so smooth one day and then, everything can be upside down the next. I have found over the years that even the darkest of clouds eventually shows a silver lining. Even the most difficult experiences teach us something or give us important insight and clarity. Of course, we hate it when we are going through it, but life's trials seem to deepen our wells of wisdom and gratitude. Although you may be in a dark period that seems to have no redeeming purpose at present, if you look back at past difficulties and remember the gift that eventually emerged, you may feel heartened in your ability to go forward and believe that it will get better and that we will always be given what we need.

On the left side of the lines below, list the event or relationship that caused you emotional pain. On the right, share the gift that eventually emerged. It is my hope that you will find this process encouraging and enlightening. Feel free to do this on a separate sheet of paper, or a poster board if you prefer.

Pain   Payoff

1._____

2._____

3._____

4._____

5._____

6._____

7._____

8._____

9._____

10._____

The Head and Heart Breath

This is a little breath with a powerful punch that I developed to help calm and center you in a simple, easy to remember way. It is especially helpful when you are feeling pulled in a thousand directions and can't think straight. It calms and brings body and mind into calm alignment.

Place the middle fingers of one hand on the side of the eye at the Gallbladder Meridian point, right on the bone on the side of the eye. The three fingers of the other hand are on the Conception 19 point in the center of the sternum on the upper chest, a bit lower than the collarbones. Cross your ankles, close your eyes and simply breathe. This breath synchronizes the energy and calms the body.

EMOTIONAL OVERLOAD CALMING PROCESS

Created by Donna Eden, *Energy Medicine*

Separating Heaven and Earth

This exercise is a powerful stretch that opens the meridians, expels toxic energies and stimulates fresh energy to flow through the joints.

1. Stand with your hands on your thighs, fingers spread.

2. With a deep inhalation through your nose, circle your arms out, having your hands meet at chest level, fingers touching in prayer position. Exhale through your mouth.

3. Again, with a deep inhalation through your nose, separate your arms from one another, stretching one high above your head and flattening your hand back, as if pushing something above you. Stretch the other arm down, again flattening your hand back, as if pushing something toward the earth. Hold this position as long as possible.

4. Then release your breath through your mouth, returning your hands into the prayer position. Repeat, switching the arm that raises and the arm that lowers. Do one or more additional lifts on each side.

5. Coming out of this pose as you bring your arm down, allow your body to fold over at the waist. Hang there with your knees slightly bent as you take two deep breaths.

6. Slowly return to a standing position, with a backward roll of the shoulders.

Neurovascular Holding Points

These points affect blood circulation. By softly holding these points when under stress, overwhelmed or in a highly emotional state, the energy from your fingertips will keep the blood from leaving your forebrain. This will help you to think more clearly and calm down.

1. Lightly place your fingertips on your forehead, covering the frontal eminences, the "Oh my God" points.
2. Put your thumbs on your temples next to your eyes, breathing deeply.
3. As the blood returns to the forebrain over the next few minutes, you will find yourself beginning to think more clearly. It's that simple.

Smoothing Behind the Ears

This process traces a portion of Triple Warmer Meridian backwards, sedating the meridian and creating a calming affect.

1. Breathe in deeply, going from the above position (Neurovascular holding points.) to smoothing the skin from the points over the temples to above the ears.
2. On the exhalation, circle your fingers around your ears, draw them down the sides of your neck, and hang your hands on the backs of your shoulders, pressing your fingers into your shoulders.
3. Stay in this position through at least two deep breaths. Then drag your fingers slowly over your shoulders with pressure. Once your fingers reach your clavicle, cross your hands over the heart chakra and take 3 easy breaths.

Solar Plexus Center Balancers

These activities help to energize and balance this center, which focuses on the self. It is very important to engage in self-care at this time. Eating right, sleeping enough, exercising and other nurturing, restorative activities are critical if we are to have the stamina to do the work of healing emotional pain.

- Spend time in bright, radiant sunlight, feeling its warmth on your skin.
- Visualize the color yellow swirling in the center of your stomach. Wear yellow clothing.
- Exercises and Yoga Postures that activate the stomach area like Curls and the Plank, the Bow, the Tree and the Cobra poses.
- Aromatherapy using, Ylang Ylang, Vetivert, Mint, Frangipani, or Clove.
- Chant "Ram"
- Wear Gemstones such as Amber, Golden Citrine, Howlite, Jasper, Labradorite, Sunstone, Tiger Eye and Topaz.
- Eat yellow foods like Summer Squash, Pears, Bananas, Lemons, Yellow Bell Peppers, Golden Apples, Yellow Lentils and Complex Carbohydrates.
- Listen to powerful, strong, assertive music such as Beethoven and Wagner.
- Meditation using the Solar Plexus Center Mudra. Thumbs are crossed and tucked between hands in Prayer Position extended from Solar Plexus.
- Massaging the middle toe and finger.

EFT Tapping Suggestions

Again, after determining what your SUDS is on a specific issue, tap on all the points shown in the chart in Chapter Two (pg. 71) As examples of the kinds of things you would tap on in this phase, here are some statements:

1. "Even though I feel alone and incapable of dealing with this, I deeply and completely accept myself." Then tap all the points saying, "Alone and incapable."

2. "Even though no one seems to care and it makes me angry, I...." Then tap all the points saying, "No one cares and I'm angry."

3. "Even though this just feels too big for me, I..." Then tap all the points saying, "Too big, can't handle it."

4. "Even though I can't seem to do anything consistently, I..." Then tapping all the points say, "Can't be consistent."

5. "Even though I don't want to be with anybody, I..." Tapping all of the points, say "I don't want to be with anyone."

After doing several rounds assess your SUDS and repeat the statement or adjust it to be more specific to what you are feeling.

When you feel you have reached a 0, think of a positive condition you would like to be experiencing and tap that into all of the points in 3 rounds. Here is an example: "I feel supported, strong and capable."

Journaling

Journaling

_____
_____
_____
_____
_____
_____
_____
_____
_____
_____
_____
_____
_____
_____
_____
_____
_____
_____
_____
_____
_____
_____
_____
_____

Journaling

CHAPTER SIX

The Long and Winding Road

"Many times I've been alone, many times I've cried."

The Beatles (*The Long and Winding Road*)

The Energy: Emotional, Introspective, Contemplative, Both Expanded and Contracted –
Relating to the Heart Energy Center or Chakra

The Action: Listen to your heart. Feel the feelings that are coming up for you. Express those feelings honestly and authentically. Don't be afraid to experience joy and laughter. Spend time in quiet, contemplative activities such as meditation and journaling.

The roller coaster of emotional pain is unpredictable when you are dealing with loss and life transitions. You may be quietly sobbing one moment and engaged in angry outbursts the next. This unpredictable, erratic energy can also show itself as explosions of uncontrollable laughter, or even sudden feelings of joy and wellbeing. These emotions need to be expressed, hopefully as productively as possible, and then allowed to move on and dissipate. In this way, we keep moving forward through our pain and don't get stuck in complicated behavior patterns created by unexpressed grief.

Expressing feelings rather than pushing them down is very important. Listen to your inner voice. It is essential to take time to go within and see what's there every day. This may be a time when you access the depths of your pain and end up crying needed tears, or more often, just a quiet time when you are truly present in the moment, experiencing peace.

An interesting thing that I have observed is that when one is in the moment, there usually is no sadness or grief. The reason for this is that emotional pain is pretty much dependent on mental trips into the past and into the future in order to be created. You need to go into the past, access a memory and then get upset about not being able to experience this anymore, in order to feel emotional pain. Or you go into the future and think about a future circumstance without the person, place or thing you have lost, allowing you to feel anxiety, sadness or fear.

However, when you are just breathing and concentrating on a sound or a focal point, you are present in the now and rarely does sadness or pain exist in the present moment. When you find yourself reaching into the past or future and feeling painful emotions, it is helpful to take a breath and pull yourself back into the present, then find a thought about the present that feels better. This takes practice, but it is such a valuable, self-loving tool, that it is well worth the effort.

Honoring and allowing our emotional state on a daily basis is the productive, growth-full way to stay in touch with our feelings and keep our systems healthy and clear. Unfortunately, what happens all too often is that we are afraid to express our emotions as they arise, or we are in circumstances that don't allow us to express them. So, we repress the emotions until the system can't hold anymore and it finally cracks from the pressure. This cracking can show up in many different ways. It can become addictive behaviors, depression, anxiety, an inability to focus, illness, or a host of other emotional disorders.

The irony is that the answer really is so simple. Thoughts and sensory experiences create emotional energy. Once that is present, it needs to be released. If we feel it and release it, we are fine to go forward. If we don't, we become burdened with needing to use our available energy to hold the emotional energy down and keep it at bay.

It's kind of like a snapshot of an excruciating, painful moment. The kind of snapshot we might build a filing system to store, simply so that we don't have to look at it anymore. The only flaw in this clever plan is that unexpected occurrences can cause it to pop up again. When it does, the emotion is as fresh as if it had just happened, and now we have to go through the pain all over again.

What most people don't realize is that if we can just experience the emotion and let it pass through, it is completed and we no longer have to expend energy holding it at bay or trying not to feel it. This requires courage, but I promise you, feeling and expressing the pain is far less difficult than using masses of energy to push it down or away.

Even when we are grieving, we are capable of laughter and it is incredibly important for us to engage in laughter as often as possible. Actively seek out your fun, funny friends. Listen to comedy channels, or rent funny movies. Laughter is a very high vibration and it gets the energy moving. This is what we want. Stuck energy is not your friend at this point.

Sometimes clients tell me that when they laugh or, God forbid, have fun, they actually feel guilty, especially if someone they loved has died or been hurt. This is normal, but not productive. No one that loves you would ever deny you a moment of joy, so don't deny it to yourself out of guilt or false loyalty. Remember, the purpose of life is joy. And to have a moment of joy in the midst of pain helps you remember why life is worth living.

This is the time to start exploring forgiveness, because if we don't let the pain, anger, frustration and hatred go, we remain imprisoned by the intense energy of those heavy feelings.

Do I have to forgive in order to heal? This is a powerful question and my answer is that while forgiveness is a powerful action to take, it is not essential that it be enacted in the traditional sense, in order to have healing occur. One doesn't always have to issue forgiveness in a way that implies understanding and condoning. You know, the 'forgive and forget' approach. In some extreme cases, all that may be realistic is for the injured person is to acknowledge what happened and express the hurt feelings that resulted. After having expressed the pain, the next step is to make a conscious choice not to let those feelings hurt you anymore. This requires actively choosing a thought that feels better, each time the hurt, angry feelings emerge. There is an in-depth piece on forgiveness, which follows. Please read it and give it serious attention.

Heart Center Energy

The Heart Center is the most powerful energy center in the human energy system, because it is the center from which we experience our emotional life. Without our emotional life, we would be boring, lifeless beings. Our feelings are what create the interest and window dressing of life.

The Heart Center is also the home of love and love is the most beautiful, powerful energy in the Universe. I don't think any of us would want to experience life without love. It is what creates joy, drama, motivation, passion and pretty much all of our other emotions, as well.

This arena is the central powerhouse of the human energy system. Through this center, it is possible to experience oneness with life and a connection with Divine, unconditional love. It is the center of love, compassion, forgiveness, empathy, openness and nurturing ability. It has the critical function of connecting us with others through emotions.

For all of these reasons, it is the most highly activated center when we are experiencing loss and life transition. The entire experience is really about what we are feeling, and this center is the point of origin for those feelings. Because the Heart Center is so active when we are in this erratic emotional time, it is very important to take good care of it. Methods for balancing and energizing the Heart Center follow later in this chapter.

In the cutting edge work done by *Heart Math,* a non-profit institute, whose mission is to transform lives through helping people bring their physical, mental and emotional systems into balanced alignment with their heart's intuitive guidance. Through their cutting edge research, they have proven scientifically that the heart has a great deal of neural tissue and works very powerfully with the brain. This center has the potential to unite all living things in peace and love through the phenomena of coherence, which is achieved when we are feeling and thinking in a positive way. A powerful Heart Math process to achieve coherence is included in your work for this phase.

Read:

Forgiveness, The Key to Emotional Freedom (pg. 104) Do I Have to Forgive? (pg. 107)

Processes to Do:

The Dear John and Beyond Letter (pg.110) Quick Coherence Technique, (pg. 113) PEP (pg. 115) Heart Center Balancing processes (pg. 116) EFT (pg. 117)

Quick Coherence

PEP

EFT

Journal:

Regarding your experiences while praying and meditating. What, if any, issues do you have around forgiveness? How were you raised to think about forgiveness? Who do you need to forgive, and for what? Is there anybody that you would like to have forgive you? Can you understand how not forgiving keeps you imprisoned?

FORGIVENESS

The Key to Emotional Freedom

"Forgiveness is the fragrance the violet leaves behind on the foot that crushed it."

Anonymous

When we have relationships that caused or still cause us considerable pain, the pain can lead to the formation of resentments, anxiety, fears, frustration and ongoing anger. Most of the time, the key to completing this pain and moving on, is FORGIVENESS.

The act of forgiving can release us from the self-imposed imprisonment that occurs when hatred and resentment obsess us. Yes, as long as we dwell on the hurts perpetrated by another human being, and as long as we need them to say or do something in order for us to feel better; we are on some level, imprisoned by them. We become victims, unable to create the kind of lives we really want. This is equally true with situations that we obsess upon and feel must be changed before we can let go of the hurt and move on.

Rarely does it happen, that someone says or does, that particular thing we think we need them to say or do, so we can let go and forgive. It almost never happens that a circumstance conforms exactly to our desires, changing in just the way we need it to. This leaves us doomed to remain victims, until we can find another way out. In my opinion, the only way out is through forgiveness. If we take the responsibility to forgive, accept people as they are and give up futile expectations, we have a much better prospect of happily going forward with our lives. We take back the power over our lives, which was given up when we became imprisoned by our obsession with the wrongs committed.

Forgiveness is one of the most misunderstood concepts that there is. In Aramaic, the ancient language of the Bible, forgiveness is defined as "Letting go of needing things to be the way we want them to be."

So many people believe that forgiveness is synonymous with condoning. This is far from the truth. Forgiveness doesn't necessarily mean that what was done is ok. That could be part of forgiveness, but it isn't implicit.

Really, forgiveness is something we do to let ourselves out of the prison of our anger and resentment. Holding onto grudges, resentments and anger robs us of our energy and keeps what little energy we have vibrating at a very low, slow level.

To avoid giving our perpetrators power over our futures, we have three basic steps that we must take.

1. Acknowledge who the perpetrator was and express the pain and anger felt.
2. Forgive them to whatever extent we can.
3. Go forward taking our eyes off the past.

Please pay attention to the order in which I stated that these actions should occur. I didn't say forgive them, as the first action. I said acknowledge and express the pain and anger first. It is my belief that most people can't forgive because they haven't done this part fully.

We have to get real clear about the injustice perpetrated and express it honestly, not politely, honestly. Then we can work with our energy system to clear the frequency of the long held feelings and make a space for forgiveness to occur. In all likelihood, this will not happen all at once. Forgiveness is a process just like grief is. You have to go through your own set of unique experiences before you can move to the stage where true forgiveness is possible.

The whole idea is to just open up to the value and importance of forgiveness, and open to taking the actions necessary to free yourself from the prison of past hurts. This will free you to step out of victimhood and into your power in the present moment.

Sometimes, when the hurts are very deep or past training makes it impossible to use the words "I forgive" it can be helpful to substitute the following sentence; "I am clear about the things you did or didn't do that hurt me, I have expressed them honestly and I am not going to let them run my life anymore."

Remember, to forgive doesn't mean that an action is condoned or even that we will forget it. What it does mean is that we are making a pro-active choice to free ourselves from the pain that holding onto the feelings, creates within us. This is powerful and the energy of that power can produce miraculous results.

You may have lost a loved one whom you feel needs no forgiveness. They may have died or had to move away. If this is the case, before you abandon the idea of forgiveness, see if perhaps you need to forgive them for having left you, even if you know they had no choice, some part of you may be hurt that they abandoned you.

Sometimes, the forgiveness you need to issue is to yourself. We all tend to be so intolerant of our own mistakes or actions. Remember, implicit in the word "human" is the word "imperfection". None of us has mastered perfection. But most of us, most of the time, are doing the absolute best we can with who we are and what we know at the moment. Don't burden yourself with unnecessary guilt. It is not a productive use of your energy as you journey toward healing.

DO I HAVE TO FORGIVE?

Forgiveness is a very important action and concept on the path to healing from grief. Forgiveness can be a springboard to healing because it clears away the resentments and hatred that block our energy and imprison us emotionally.

People often ask me: Do I have to forgive in order to heal? This is a powerful question and my answer is that while it is a powerful action to take, it is not essential to forgive in the traditional sense in order to have a healing impact. What I am saying is that one doesn't have to issue forgiveness in a way that implies understanding and condoning, there doesn't need to be a "forgive and forget" type approach. Some acts are so cruel and have inflicted so much pain that for a person to get to forgiveness feels nearly impossible. In such a case, all that may be realistic is for the injured person to acknowledge what happened and express the hurt feelings that resulted. After having done this, the next step is to make a conscious choice not to let those feelings hurt you anymore. Doing this in an effective way requires a safe environment wherein you fully express the anger, hurt, frustration, hatred, resentment or whatever other emotions were produced by the actions of the perpetrator. After that has happened, an energetic space can open up to allow the action of choosing something different; not to let these things eat you up and own you anymore.

There is another aspect of forgiveness that also needs to be explored. Is it always incumbent upon us to forgive? In an article entitled, *Do I Have To Forgive?,* author Richard P. Lord, says,

> "*Dietrich Bonhoeffer wrote that 'cheap grace' is the preaching of forgiveness without requiring repentance. Repentance has traditionally involved three aspects,*

which guard against cheap grace: Remorse, Restitution, and Regeneration.

First a genuine 'I'm sorry' is required. Remorse is integral to forgiveness being appropriate.

Second, insofar as possible an attempt must be made to restore what was destroyed. This means accepting legal, financial and moral consequences.

Third, there must be renewal, a change in how the person lives."

Without these three aspects present, Lord feels that forgiveness isn't even appropriate, and certainly not deserved.

When these three aspects are present, forgiveness is a powerful action to take. However, even then, it still may only be possible to do what we described above; basically saying, "I acknowledge the things you did or didn't do that hurt me, and I'm not going to let them hurt me any more."

Whether you choose to do it this way or to forgive in the more traditional way, it is highly advisable to first express the hurt feelings and acknowledge what happened before moving on to the act of forgiveness. Too often, people try to forgive before having thoroughly expressed their pain, and the result is not what they desired.

Taking either of these kinds of actions will lead to the ultimate goal of forgiveness: to release you from the imprisonment created by holding onto hatred and resentments. Yes, as long as we dwell on the hurts perpetrated by another human being and need that person to do or say something in order for us to feel better; we are on some level imprisoned by them. We become victims, unable to create the kind of lives we really want. What makes this position even more pathetic is the fact that rarely do people ever do or say what we think we need to hear in order to forgive them. We need to take back our power through expression of pain and consciously choosing to release the resentments, thereby also releasing ourselves.

If we forgive an act; it doesn't mean that what was done is okay. It doesn't mean that all is forgotten. It simply means that we have made a conscious decision not to focus our energy on the negative emotions created by the pain inflicted upon us. It means we are taking back the power to create our lives the way we want them to be, no longer victim to anyone's cruelty.

You may find that some of the forgiveness you need to issue will be to yourself. Remember that most of us, most of the time, are doing the absolute best we can with who we are, and what we are and know in the moment. Don't burden yourself with unnecessary guilt. It is not a productive use of your energy as you journey toward healing.

DEAR JOHN AND BEYOND

FORGIVENESS LETTER

(concept originally explored by John James, *The Grief Recovery Handbook*)

Dear John

Those two words are famous (some might say infamous) for signaling the ending of a relationship. They immediately conjure up a sense of dread; somebody is going to get some bad news. However, endings are not always a negative experience, especially if the relationship has been one of pain. When we are dealing with loss, the relationship is always one that involves pain. Even if the relationship had been great before the loss, since the loss, it has been one of pain. This agony is often eased or alleviated by the expression of certain thoughts and feelings in the right kind of letter. This version of a "Dear John" can be very healing.

Let's talk about the kind of things that need to be discussed in a letter that will help you heal. After reading this piece, please write this letter to the person, place or circumstance that you have lost.

1. First of all, you must tell the truth about what existed in the relationship. Remember, all relationships have both positive and negative aspects. That is what we need to talk about in the first part of this letter. What were the aspects of the relationship that upset or bothered you? What were the things you wish had been different? What were the good parts that you cherish and wouldn't change? Discuss those in detail.

2. Secondly, discuss anything you feel that you need to say you are sorry for. Talk about what happened, explain whatever you wish to and then say the words, "I'm sorry." This is an important chance to make amends. Remember, energy can't be created or destroyed. The body of energy or life force that animated the person you have lost, exists, even if there has been a death. This energy is present to receive this letter. So let yourself off the hook. Apologize sincerely and know that you can move on now.

3. Next, we need to look at any forgiveness that needs to be issued or received. As we have discussed before, forgiveness can be a springboard for healing. Remember, the process of forgiveness really focuses on you, not the person you need to forgive. It's really all about you asking for forgiveness, if you feel you need to, and about you issuing forgiveness when necessary, to release yourself from the imprisonment of hatred and resentment. In prior discussions, we also said that forgiveness doesn't always have to be done in the traditional way, where it is implied that all is understood and forgotten. It can also take the form of the statement "I acknowledge what you did or didn't do that hurt me and I am choosing not to let it hurt me any more." It is also important to remember that you may need to issue forgiveness to yourself in this letter. This self-forgiveness can be important to acknowledge in conjunction with the relationship you are focusing on.

The bottom line is that forgiveness is a release of all the energy that has become stuck in the slow, painful vibration of hatred and resentment. Once this happens, the energy is vibrant, flowing and available for you to use again.

4. Gratitude is another concept we have been working with throughout this book. Gratitude is an excellent way to raise your vibration to a very high level, which accelerates your healing. So look at the relationship you have lost and see what you are grateful for. What events and experiences blessed your life? What changed you and helped you grow?

5. Say "goodbye." This can be accompanied with "I miss you, I love you," or other such words, if that feels right to you. But definitely say the words "goodbye." This is not good-bye forever; it is simply a way of ending the present interaction. In our culture, this is what we say to signify the ending of a communication. It doesn't mean that there won't be more communications; it just means that you are complete with this one. Often times, the writing of this letter alleviates so much pain, that it opens up an ongoing dialogue with a loved one, that was not possible before because it was too painful.

We are also saying goodbye to any pain associated with the relationship. We may be saying goodbye to the hopes and dreams that things will ever be any different or better than they actually were. And we are saying goodbye to the physical person that no longer interacts with us on a daily basis. We are not, however, saying goodbye to the emotional or spiritual aspects of the relationship that we treasure, as these will continue. The primary purpose of saying goodbye is to COMPLETE the painful aspects of the relationship so that we are free to create our lives the way we want them to be and to be present in the moment to experience them.

THE QUICK COHERANCE TECHNIQUE

Created by Don Childre, The Heart Math Institute

Quick Coherence is a powerful technique for refocusing your emotions, connecting you with your energetic heart zone, and releasing stress. Cumulative stress creates a cloud of incoherence. By practicing the Quick Coherence technique, you increase self-alignment, drawing in more of your higher discernment faculties and increasing access to your intuition. Heart coherence increases operative intuition for day-to-day facilitation and guidance. Once learned, the Quick Coherence technique only takes a minute to do. It consists of three easy steps: Heart Focus, Heart Breathing and Heart Feeling. After doing these steps, it often becomes clear what the best course of action would be in a given situation.

Step 1. Heart Focus or Freeze Frame

Shift your attention to the area of the heart, or the center of your chest.

If you don't understand how, try this: Focus on your right big toe and wiggle it. Now focus on your right elbow. Now gently focus in the center of your chest, the area of your heart. If you lose focus, just keep shifting your attention back to the area of your heart. Now you're ready for the next step, Heart Breathing.

Step 2: Heart Breathing.

Breathe slow and deeply. Imagine the air entering and leaving through the heart area, or the center of your chest.

Heart Breathing helps you begin to get in sync and draws the energy out of the head, where negative thoughts and feelings are amplified. This helps neutralize stressful feelings. If it's hard to disengage from stressful feelings, don't worry. Just really wanting to disengage can help you release a lot of emotional energy.

Step 3: Heart Feeling.

Remember a time when you felt good inside and try to re-experience that feeling. Focus on this good feeling as you continue to breathe through the area of your heart. This could be a feeling of appreciation toward a special person or a pet, a place you enjoy, or an activity that was fun.

This is the key step to getting and staying in sync. Many people find that when they experience positive feelings like care, love, or appreciation while breathing through the heart area, they immediately feel and think better. Holding a positive feeling makes it easier to stay in sync for longer periods of time, so that it becomes easier to remain calm and balanced even in tough times. Now, in this calm, clear state, ask your heart what the best course of action is.

With the Quick Coherence technique, it takes only a minute to get in sync and reduce stress right in the moment. It takes some practice, but it is absolutely worth it.

You can do Quick Coherence anytime, anyplace and no one knows you are doing it.

Key Points:

You can apply this one-minute technique first thing in the morning, during work or school, in the middle of a difficult conversation, when you feel overloaded or pressed for time, or any time you simply want to get in sync.

Athletes use Quick Coherence whenever they need to boost their energy levels, coordination, reaction times, and speed while playing sports. The Military, Police and Firemen use Quick Coherence to maintain alertness and the ability to think quickly on their feet, especially in extreme situations.

Quick Coherence can help you perform better on tests, help you get along better with others, and relax and calm down when you are feeling anxious or stressed.

PEP- Lung Meridian Breathing for Clearing Emotional Pain and Limiting Beliefs

Created by Phil Mollon, Ph.D.

This process is one of my favorite, simple, yet powerful tools for clearing unproductive behaviors, feelings and limiting beliefs.

1. Cross hands over chest and place fingertips on the Lung Alarm Points, which are in front of the armpits. You know you are on them when you lift your elbows and feel a hollow area. Now relax you elbows back down.

2. Hold the intention of clearing the belief or issue while your fingertips are resting on the Lung Alarm Points. Speak silently or out loud, "I release…." (state what you desire to release).

3. Breathe deeply and evenly.

4. As you breathe, speak the words, silently or out loud, "Releasing all the thoughts and energy fields, including all the roots and origins that are holding this problem, issue, or behavior in place." Continue holding the points and breathing until you feel a shift.

   I often continue holding the points after feeling the shift and then program into my being a positive state that I now want to exist. (e.g. "I am peaceful and at ease.")

Heart Center Balancers

It is important to keep this center strong, as it is probably the one most impacted by loss. The activities below will assist you in keeping this center open, strong, active and able to handle the rigors of emotional turmoil inherent in grief.

- Spend time in a lush, green setting, especially one that might include pink flowers.
- Visualize the color Green swirling in the area of the heart. Wear green clothing.
- Exercises and Yoga Postures that activate the area of the heart, like push ups, shoulder rolls, the Camel, Cat Pose, and the Sphinx poses.
- Aromatherapy with Rose, Jasmine or Lavender.
- Chant "Yahm"
- Wear Gemstones such as Emerald, Green Aventurine, Jade, Malachite Moonstone, Rose Quartz, and Watermelon Tourmaline.
- Eat green foods such as Lettuce, Broccoli, Kale, Zucchini, and Green Apples.
- Listen to melodic beautiful music like Mozart, Bach and Debussy.
- Meditation using the Heart Center Mudra. Connect the tips of the thumbs and middle fingers and rest hands in the lap.
- Massaging the first toe or index finger.

EFT Tapping Suggestions

Again, after determining what your SUDS is on a specific issue, tap on all the points shown in the chart in Chapter Two (pg. 71) As examples of the kinds of things you would tap on in this phase, here are some statements:

1. "Even though I feel emotional pain all the time and it seems like it will never end, I deeply and completely accept myself." Then tap all the points saying, "Pain that never ends."

2. "Even though no one wants to hear about my pain, I...." Then tap all the points saying, "No one wants to hear my pain."

3. "Even though I try to forgive but can't let go of the hatred and anger, I...." Then tap all the points saying, "Can't let go of the hatred and anger."

4. "Even though I am on the edge of tears all the time, I...." Then tap all the points saying, "Edge of tears all the time."

5. "Even though I don't know how to find joy anymore, I...." Tapping all of the points

saying, "Can't find joy anymore."

After doing several rounds, assess your SUDS and repeat the statement or adjust it to be more specific to what you are feeling.

When you feel you have reached a 0, think of a positive condition you would like to be experiencing and tap that into all of the points in 3 rounds. Here is an example: "I accept my feelings and will allow myself the time and healing I need."

Journaling

_____

_____

_____

_____

_____

_____

_____

_____

_____

_____

_____

_____

_____

_____

_____

_____

_____

_____

_____

_____

_____

_____

_____

_____

Journaling

_____

_____

_____

_____

_____

_____

_____

_____

_____

_____

_____

_____

_____

_____

_____

_____

_____

_____

_____

_____

_____

_____

_____

_____

_____

Journaling

CHAPTER SEVEN

I Want To Tell You

"I want to tell you, my head is full of things to say."

The Beatles (*I Want to Tell You*)

The Energy: Expressive, Communicative, Outwardly Focused, Relating to the Throat Energy Center or Chakra.

The Action: Speak your truth and let others know what you need, what you feel, what you desire and what you are uncomfortable with.

Express your thoughts about the way you want to be treated, helped and allowed to process your own feelings. Don't be afraid to tell the truth. Remember, you're the one who is in pain! The Energy is intense and needing to be expressed, not suppressed.

In a culture that thinks it makes sense to give a person three days off from work after the death of a significant someone in his or her life, it is not easy to be honest or to express your self authentically, after a difficult life transition. In fact, if a person in emotional pain is to function at all in this culture, it is pretty much imperative that they master an acceptable social facade.

How can one be authentic when the only way to function three days after a significant loss is to put on the "I'm fine" face and try to bravely carry out the doings of a normal day? All the while, praying that you will be able to hold it together, contain your real emotions, and pull off the pretense one more time?

Day after day, this grueling charade takes its toll on the physical, mental and emotional bodies. It takes energy to hold back what is real. Using your energy in this way zaps you of what you need for healing and for the other activities of your daily life. You end up feeling tired all the time and life becomes an arduous chore.

Besides the cultural pressure that drives us underground when we are in emotional pain, our own misinformed ideas often do the same. We think we should "be over it by now." Or we feel ashamed and defective that we can't seem to get it together, so we pretend that we are okay.

Many people don't express their true thoughts and feelings because they fear that if they let them go they won't be able to pull them back and regain control. They hide behind the mask of "I'm fine" until they can get home, pull down the shades and allow the real self to emerge. Many of them do this in shame, feeling weak and somehow defective, instead of honoring their right to express the pain they feel.

One of the worst aspects of suppressing emotions is that to do so is completely unnatural. As I stated at the beginning of the book, the word emotion comes from the Latin words for "move" and "out." Emotions are all about moving you and moving out. This natural process only happens when we feel them and express them.

Loss can break you in half, beat you down and tear your heart out. The pain or intense discomfort can become such a problem that we unconsciously fall into thought patterns or behaviors that distract us, often creating problems that are far more difficult to deal with than the emotional pain that preceded them. Many people turn to practices that either anesthetize the pain or distract them from it. These behaviors can become addictive and can monopolize your life and eventually destroy it.

Addiction is a major problem among humans and the reason for this is simple. We abhor pain and if we have no skills for healing and shifting our pain, we will do whatever seems necessary to alleviate it for a time. The tools from Mind/Body Medicine that I work with are simple and effective. They don't mask or temporarily reduce emotional pain. They actually change it, so that life can be lived joyfully and choice-fully.

Drinking too much, using drugs, sex, work, gambling, shopping, or exercise are ways that we distract ourselves from the fact that our broken hearts are hurting and that pain causes us to feel fearful, anxious, depressed, angry, hopeless and overwhelmed.

The problem however, is that when we repress, deny, or deaden our feelings, we ultimately destroy much of our capacity to enjoy life, living, and loving, because we cannot relate to others, if we don't feel.

Throat Center Energy

The Throat Center is the center of expression. Speaking your truth and expressing your feelings are the main jobs of this energy center. When one is hurting, this function is often difficult and not done as easily and openly as would be beneficial.

As I have mentioned before, feelings and emotions are designed to be acknowledged, felt, expressed and moved through. When this doesn't happen, complicated psychological structures form to suppress, dismiss or deny those feelings.

It never ceases to amaze me how powerful it is to express one's feelings and one's truth. Conversely, it is equally amazing to see how damaging the effects of truth and feelings suppressed can be.

One of the reasons that it can be difficult to express our pain is that we feel forsaken by God, and the Throat Center is about lessons of our will versus Divine will. Whether it's because we have been taught to fear God or we have just become numbed by our pain, too many people don't use the immense healing tool of verbal expression.

We've all had the experience of finally getting something off our chests and feeling much lighter and happier as a result. When you are dealing with loss, the total focus of life is about those painful things that resulted from the loss. If we can't express that pain it gets stuck at the throat and can manifest in a number of ways. How many of you have chronic neck and shoulder pain? This is just one manifestation of blocked energy.

The nature of energy is expansive, it requires outward motion or it will just circle itself and stay stuck. Speaking and releasing the emotional nature of your pain is critical to healing. Here are some articles and processes to assist you in this endeavor.

Read:

Grief Avoidance Response Mechanisms (pg. 165) Relationships - The Good, The Bad and The Interesting (pg. 170)

Processes To Do:

Energy Circles (pg. 173), Let it Go, Let it Go, Let it Go (pg. 175), Read the Dear John Letter Out Loud to a Trusted Friend, Throat Center Balancing Processes (pg. 177) EFT (pg. 178)

Energy Circles   EFT

Journal:

After reading the pieces on Grief Avoidance Responses and about your own experiences with Grief Avoidance Response Mechanisms. Are there some that have become problematic or perhaps helpful in some way? Have you had to deal with any in the past that are rearing their ugly heads now? What can you do instead of engaging in Grief Avoidance Responses? Are you able to see the relationship lost in a balanced way? Did doing the exercise help? How?

GRIEF AVOIDANCE RESPONSE MECHANISMS

Intense pain and grief is a normal, natural response to loss, but it can also be devastating. The pain is sometimes so intense that you don't know how you are going to take your next breath.

Many people turn to behaviors that either anesthetize the pain or distract them from it. These behaviors can become addictive. They can monopolize your life and eventually destroy it.

Why do we try so hard to sidetrack ourselves from our pain? Why do we deny, yet fight for our right, to "check out" in whatever way we have chosen to? The answer is very obvious: nobody likes pain and way too many people have no idea what to do to process the pain and actually heal. So the best that they think they can do, is to find some way to reduce the amount of pain being felt in the moment. The job of taking the focus off the pain is accomplished in many ways. The problem is that most of these methods that are used to avoid pain, end up creating even more pain, often destroying one's life and hurting loved ones.

If some of the below behaviors are too familiar to you, you may be at risk and should really seek professional help to deal with your grief and the resulting addictive behavior.

If you have become:

1. The CHEMICAL ABUSER
2. The DRINKER
3. The WORKER
4. The SHOPPER
5. The POSTPONER
6. The DISPLACER
7. The REPLACER
8. The MINIMIZER
9. The SOMATICIZER
10. The EATER
11. The TRAVELER
12. The CRUSADER
13. The INTERNET PORN USER
14. The OBSESSIVE EXERCISER
15. The OBSESSIVE VIDEO OR CARD GAME PLAYER
16. The TELEVISION ADDICT

You may be using these behaviors to avoid the pain of the loss that you are experiencing. All of these behaviors can be Grief Avoidance Mechanisms, or addictions, as we commonly refer to them.

All Grief Avoidance Response Mechanisms have the same subconscious purpose; temporary relief from the pain caused by loss. The problem however, is that when we repress, deny, or deaden our feelings, we ultimately become destructive to ourselves.

Grief and Addictions

All addiction has grief underneath it. This is why we refer to addictions as Grief Avoidance Response Mechanisms. As we previously stated, the purpose that addiction serves in the grief process is distraction from pain.

Because there is so much loss in life, there are a lot of people in this world who are hurting. I think that there is a Universal agreement that pain sucks, so we end up with a lot of people looking for a way to feel better.

Let's look a little more closely at loss, which always precedes grief. Loss is the experience of having a treasured person, place, experience, relationship, circumstance or object removed from your life experience.

Types of Loss

Financial Loss, Job Loss, Divorce, Animal Friend Loss, Divorce, Ending of a Relationship, Loss of Health or Physical Appearance, Loss of Body Parts or Functions, Home Loss, Moving, Loss of Youth, Loss of Treasured Object, Loss of Treasured Place, Retirement, Alzheimer's Disease, Life Style Loss, Marriage, Job Change, Loss of a Treasured Situation, Loss of Security, Loss of Identity, Loss of Notoriety.

This list is hardly comprehensive, and still you can see that it's pretty difficult to get through a day without some type of loss occurring.

Addictions are tough to heal because we develop them on two levels.

A. Psychological Addiction – When one is addicted to the feelings produced by doing certain practices.

B. Physiological Addiction – When the cells of the body prefer the chemicals provided by the addiction, to nutrition.

As Dr. Candace Pert taught us in her book, *Molecules of Emotions*, what actually happens is that emotions prompt the production of certain chemicals within the brain that are connected with that given emotion. We have receptor sites for these chemicals on all of the cells in the body. When the blood is flooded with these chemicals over and over again, the cells begin to prefer them to other forms of nutrition, and consequently, develop an addiction to them.

The scientific truth is that if you are sad, angry or fearful all the time, the body will develop an addiction to the chemicals produced by those emotions. Too many people become monuments to despair and lose the quality of their lives because of an unconscious, physiological quest to get the chemical fix that the body is craving. The chemicals desired are those created by the brain when the emotions connected with grief are experienced. Yes, we do get addicted to the chemicals we produce internally, just like we get addicted to chemicals we bring in from the external world.

If you are recognizing that you have become dependent on a substance or a behavior to *feel better* about your life, it could be that underneath that feeling is pain from some past loss that you never healed. Addressing this pain and healing it could very well alleviate your need for the addictive substance or behavior.

As a culture, I believe we need to reframe the way we look at addicts. They are not weak, derelict people; they are grievers in pain. They may not even be clear about the source of the original loss but I assure you, there was one. Or more likely, several. They need understanding and healing, not shame and punishment.

If you have developed a Grief Avoidance Response Mechanism, get help to deal with your grief. There is no shame in having found a way to survive your pain, but now it is time to rise above it so that you can be thriving, not just surviving.

RELATIONSHIPS

The Good, The Bad and The Interesting

When a relationship has been lost, no matter what the reason, the mind goes on a kind of automatic review of what occurred. Some of the events will be joyful and precious, others will be painful and difficult to think about. This is the normal course any given relationship will take. However, sometimes when a relationship is very heavily weighted one way or another, the memories of the relationship can become distorted.

One of the most difficult tasks of mourning is to convert the relationship from one of interactive presence to one of appropriate memory. Appropriate memory is balanced memory. Every relationship has negative and positive aspects because every human being has negative and positive aspects. In order to grieve and heal, we must have an accurate memory of who the person was. Sometimes after a loss there is a tendency to remember someone "bigger than life," this is called Enshrinement.

On the other end of the spectrum is the survivor who has totally vilified someone they have lost. This kind of thinking often happens when there has been childhood abuse, a messy divorce, or some other kind of painful situation. When pain and hatred toward the offending person is being experienced intensely, one might be inclined to forget the reasons for initially loving that person. The happy memories of the relationship become blurred by the now existing hatred.

Let's create a list depicting the reality of the relationship. This list will encompass both the negative and positive aspects and characteristics of the person and the relationship that has been lost. This process will help you to explore the relationship accurately, not slanting it toward one extreme or the other. Having this visual representation of the pros and cons of the relationship can also be very enlightening. Sometimes it is surprising to see that a relationship remembered as having been at one end of the spectrum, actually turns out to be quite balanced. Then again, sometimes a relationship remembered as balanced, appears heavily loaded with negative events when fully explored. Either way, the goal is accuracy. No relationship is totally negative or totally positive. An accurate picture will have aspects of both, and an accurate picture is vital to successful reconciliation of the loss.

Obviously, there are relationships where there has been extreme abuse. In such a case it would be understandable to view the relationship as totally negative. However, even in the case of parental sexual abuse, one of the most reprehensible acts possible, there are usually aspects of the relationship that were not totally abusive, maybe even loving.

A sexually abusive father might have been a good provider, or might have interceded in arguments with the mother. Sometimes, it may seem impossible to find anything redeeming about a person, but if one is willing to venture the exploration, something redeeming can usually be discovered. Or perhaps there is at least something that helps you understand a bit about why the person abused in the ways they did.

Though difficult, putting time into doing this search will be worthwhile in the therapeutic, healing value that it will offer.

Here is a brief example of how this exercise might look:

Positive Aspects of Dad	Negative Aspects of Dad
Good Sense of Humor	Short Tempered
Taught me to body surf	Wouldn't play catch with me
Helped us get a dog	Wouldn't take us to the park
Very Smart	Sarcastic
Fought for me with my teacher	Never came to my plays
Helped me with my math	Watched sports all weekend
Taught me to value myself	Stingy with money
Made me feel safe at night	Negative and bigoted
Believed in me	Always questioned my judgment

Chapter Seven Processes

ENERGY CIRCLES

Energy Circles are a wonderful vehicle for stating an intention, in a kinesthetic way. They are simple, powerful and fun. They can be particularly helpful with releasing disruptive behaviors, negative patterns and the sad, heavy energy of grief, as well as the visual images of traumatic events that may have created your grief.

1. Simply draw a big imaginary circle in front of you.

2. Now, using your imagination, visualization, and your body, physically put into your circle everything that you no longer want in your life. It can be illness, pain, grief, depression, stress, circumstances you no longer want, people, places, behaviors, emotional patterns, whatever. Just get it in there. As you put each thing into the circle, speak the words describing what it is out loud.

It's best to do these circles in themes; subject areas, issues, or circumstances you want to change, for instance. Don't try to put into the circle everything you don't want in every area of your life.

3. By the time you get everything that you are releasing into the circle, the energy of it will be very heavy. After all, it is being charged with all the really low vibration stuff that you no longer desire to experience.

4. Now, reach down to the bottom of the circle with both hands, and with one mighty thrust and a huge "whoosh" sound, lift the circle up and blast it out into the Universe to be transmuted into positive energy.

5. Draw another large circle and put into it all that you do want in accordance with the theme you are working with. This could be healing, health, well-being, joy, peace, material stuff, a sweetheart, even a better body if that is what you want. Get all the good stuff in there. You can already begin to feel the buzz of the high vibration you are creating inside this circle with all the wonderful things that you desire.

6. Now comes the big moment, step into the circle. Close your eyes and feel the energy. Put it on like pants and a shirt. Bask in the energy and feel all the feelings of how good it is to have everything you want! Allow yourself to absolutely wallow in the joy. Take as long as you want. You are savoring the vortex of creative power. And in a very powerful way, you are clearly telling the Universe what you want.

Do this as often as you like. It can only make your vibrational level higher and higher. Enjoy!

Let it Go, Let it Go, Let it Go

It can be very helpful to find a way to release painful circumstances or events from your life. Keeping them within you is agonizing and non-productive. Here are some suggestions of things you might do.

- Write those painful aspects or events on another piece of paper and with the Intention of releasing them from your being, burn the paper.

- Write them on a piece of lightweight wood and release it out into the ocean or some other body of water.

- You can make a strong, powerful statement of release to the Universe. Speak the things you wrote, out loud in a private place, with your hands held up to the heavens. Feel the weight of your pain being lifted off you.

- You can actually write or visualize yourself writing the words on a balloon and then releasing it to the Universe.

- If you believe in a higher power or Divine entity like God, turn it over to that being and let it be handled by the Divine. Some people do this by writing it on a piece of paper and putting it in a box they call a "God Box," which represents the place that they put all the things they no longer want to worry or obsess about. Something similar can be done with worry dolls. These are tiny dolls made in Guatemala. The legend instructs a person with many worries to tell them to each of the dolls. Then they are returned to their pouch or box, taking with them the burdens of the owner, leaving a peaceful night's rest and a lighter heart possible.

- Visualize a bowl of light in front of you that came to you from the Universe. It is waiting to take away the burden of what you are feeling. As you say each thing you have written, feel the place in your body where it resides. Focus on it and really feel the discomfort. Give some form to the feeling, color, size, shape, weight and consistency. Then, consciously allow this "thing" to flow out of you into the bowl of light. When everything has been released, say the following words powerfully, three times: "Any energy that is not in harmony with my highest good, leave me now!" After the third time, see the bowl close up into a ball of light, holding in the contents and then see it zoom away and disappear at the speed of light like the millennium falcon in Star Wars.

Throat Center Balancers

A strong Throat Center is critical to being able to speak your truth, tell others what you need and what you desire. This is a very important component of healing from grief. The following activities will strengthen and balance this center.

- Spend time outside absorbing the clear blue color of the sky. Also effective is any setting where blue water exists and reflects the sky.
- Visualize the color turquoise or sky blue swirling at the throat. Wear clothing in those colors of blue.
- Exercises or Yoga Postures that activate the neck and throat area, like shoulder shrugs, the Bridge, the Fish and the Plough poses.
- Aromatherapy using Frankincense and Myrrh.
- Chant "*Ham*"
- Wear Gemstones such as Aquamarine, Blue Topaz, Pearls, Jasper, Lapis Lazuli,
- Kyanite and Turquoise.
- Eat Blue foods like Blueberries, Kelp, Blue Raspberries and Eggplant.
- Listen to gentle music, sounds of nature, transcendent themes and Mozart concertos.
- Meditation using the Throat Center Mudra. Interlace your fingers making sure that the right index finger is on top of the left index finger. Place the thumbs together pointing up.
- Massaging the big toe or thumb

EFT Tapping Suggestions

Again, after determining what your SUDS is on a specific issue, tap on all the points shown in the chart in Chapter Two (pg. 71) As examples of the kinds of things you would tap on in this phase, here are some statements:

1. "Even though I can't find the words to express my pain, I deeply and completely accept myself." Then tap all the points saying, "No words for the pain."

2. "Even though I can't understand or accept why God would do this to me, I...." Then tap all the points saying, "Can't understand why."

3. "Even though I'm terrified about what the future holds, I...." Then tap all the points saying, "Terrified about the future."

4. "Even though I want to tell everyone to go away and leave me alone, I...." Then tapping all the points say, "Go away and leave me alone."

5. "Even though I choke up every time I try to talk about it, I...." Tapping all of the points, say "I get choked up."

After doing several rounds, assess your SUDS and repeat the statement or adjust it to be more specific to what you are feeling.

When you feel you have reached a 0, think of a positive condition you would like to experience and tap that into all of the points in 3 rounds. Here is an example: "Words flow easily as I talk to safe people about my pain."

Journaling

Journaling

Journaling

CHAPTER EIGHT

Here Comes The Sun

"Here comes the sun, little darling. And I say, it's all right."

The Beatles (*Here Comes the Sun*)

The Energy: Open, Lighter, Explorative, Intellectual, Logical, Accepting. Relating to the Brow Center or Chakra.

The Action: Begin to re-engage in life activities. Be open to new experiences. Move toward acceptance and adjustment to your new normal. Take control of thoughts and consciously lean in the direction of thinking positive thoughts.

The energy is lighter and more stable, but still needs to be amplified and supported to be able to live in this new reality. It is important at this time to find a way to reframe the thinking and focus more on seeing the current change as holding a gift, rather than it being a complete disaster.

At this point we are beginning to access a readiness to accept this time of loss as a time of growth; to actually have hope that better things are on the way. We still feel the pain that the loss brought with it, but it isn't as acute and we are more able now to use intellect and logic to deal with it.

We can begin to believe that this painful state we have been experiencing won't be a life sentence, and that other states of being, like *normal* and *happy,* can actually exist again. We are beginning to comprehend that the journey we have been taking has been a path to growth and transformation. The plea that has been a constant refrain throughout the grief, "When Will This Pain Ever End?" almost seems to finally have an answer waiting in the wings.

Only now can we put *acceptance* into practice and not just hold it as an intellectual goal that has little place in present circumstances. To be able to accept what is, can be one of the most important mental attitudes that any of us can seek to embrace in life. Yet when we are dealing with loss and life transitions, it is one of the most difficult perspectives to embrace because we hate like hell the reality that has befallen us. It isn't easy to engage fully in acceptance when what is in front of you is the unacceptable.

Acceptance is a simple concept but it isn't an easy one. All the wise teachers throughout time have taught us the value of acceptance. It promotes peace, joy, harmonious relationships, self-love and an atmosphere of mutual respect and cooperation. Although it can be difficult, it is a goal well worth working toward.

At this point in the journey, we are also much more ready for the intellectual understanding that all life experiences are energetically based. Because, remember, everything is energy vibrating at different frequencies. The most important key to remember as we work our way through the present circumstances is that we are dealing with the energy of loss, and like all energy, it can be altered and transformed. We can feel hope and optimism if we truly understand the mutability of energy.

Every one of us has experienced our energy shifting and our moods changing at some point in time. We have felt better or worse depending on the direction the energy moved. This experience provides a model, if you will, which helps us understand the mutability of energy. Once we really comprehend that energy can, and does, change, we have reason for hope. We have a basis to believe that it actually is possible for the heavy energy of loss, in which we've become immersed, to shift and become lighter and more bearable. We begin to see the very real possibility of regaining control over our lives once again. This knowledge allows us a far more empowered state than that which exists when we feel like stagnant, helpless victims of grief, in search of someone or something to blame for our misery.

Energy Medicine and other mind/body approaches are particularly effective because of this single aspect of energy; it is mutable and can be changed. Through the tools and processes of these disciplines, we can intentionally shift energy and reduce pain to the point that it no longer paralyzes us and renders us helpless. From this place, we can do the work of healing loss far more effectively and productively. It's no longer a huge stretch to believe that transforming the heavy energy of loss and regaining a level of joy is a viable possibility. We have a legitimate basis for finding comfort in the ancient words: "This too shall pass."

Many people don't realize that joy is a choice. We have so much more power than we know. We are not like frail saplings bending in the wind. We have choice about how we interpret the events of our lives and how we respond to them. Happiness has to do with the events of the outer world, but joy is a choice. Joy comes from within and does not depend upon outer circumstances. So start each day affirming that you choose joy and stand back to be amazed at how much more joy will show up in your life.

Once you have experienced a significant emotional loss, you are forever changed; your life will never be exactly as it was before. But as we have discussed, this can be a potentially positive outcome. It enables you to have new, interesting and even exciting experiences that you probably wouldn't have had before. The old normal is gone, but a new normal can now emerge. And it can be deeper, wiser, more joyful and far more grounded in gratitude and acceptance.

This new reality can be the gateway to a better quality of life than has ever existed for you before. However, for this to unfold, one must remain open and be willing for it to happen. I know that if you have experienced something as devastating as the loss of a child, this concept is really hard to grasp. There is no doubt that going forward from that kind of a loss is incredibly difficult. Yet, after healing and attaining a level of acceptance, there can be good that can be found. For instance, some of the greatest foundations and scholarship funds that help millions of people, like Newman's Own, have been created in the aftermath of child loss. These are tragedies, no question, but the gift that came out of those devastating losses has brought new hope and life to many others.

Brow Center Energy

This is the energy of intellect and intuition. It is the place where we can make huge change on the mental level with our thoughts and habits of thought. Many of us have habits of thinking that are consistently negative, pitiful, condescending or the like. The upheaval of loss brings with it the potential of being open to creating something new. The old structures have been destroyed and in their place is fertile soil for the creation of new ones.

All loss is a death and all death creates a space for something fresh and new to be born. What will you germinate in the fertile soil of your mind? What new ways of thinking or being will you birth now? Everything is possible.

It will require courage and discipline because it is so much easier to do what you've always done before and think what you've always thought before. One of the most powerful characteristics of energy is that it is always desirous of renewal and movement. Doing things differently will actually energize this center. Dare to consider new thoughts and new ways of being. This one shift can transform your life. Unleash the energy of newness and I guarantee that you will be amazed at the lightness, vitality and joy that is possible.

While the brain likes the familiarity of sameness, it only expands and develops new neural nets through consistent new activity.

I realize that pain is still a part of your life, but try this little process: Keep your thoughts coming from a positive place. Consciously think positive thoughts about everything. When a negative or painful thought creeps in, simply choose a thought that feels better and experience joy. I often advise clients to think of their happy thoughts ahead of time and have them installed in the Rolodex of their minds. Then, when painful, energy- depleting thoughts come up, they can easily and quickly access a positive one to counteract it. I strongly encourage you to play with this. We have so much more control over our thoughts than we can imagine.

In each phase, we have been building the strength and ability to get to this place and to once again experience joy most of the time. Determine that there is no randomness in life and that everything has a purpose. This loss, while painful, had a purpose in your life. Don't waste that gift. Squeeze every drop of goodness out of your pain and use it to create something beautiful.

Read:

The Magic of Meditation (pg. 190) Acceptance - Gateway to Peace (pg. 192), Thanks for the Memories (pg. 195)

Processes To Do:

Daily Meditation, Memories (pg. 198), Anchoring the Good Memories (pg. 200), Brow Balancers (pg. 202), EFT (pg. 203)

Anchoring the Good Memories   EFT

Journal:

Journal about your plan for living within this new life and choosing joy. What kinds of changes will you need to make in your thoughts and attitudes about the transition you have experienced? Talk about any problems you are experiencing between new thoughts and old attitudes and ideas about how you *should* be. Are any aspects of the new normal bringing up fear? As always write about whatever is coming up for you at this time.

THE MAGIC OF MEDITATION

"Meditation is really just quieting yourself enough

so you can get in touch with your own inner wisdom"

Louise Hay

Meditation is without a doubt the single most important, powerful, transformative practice any person can include in their lives, but for a griever, it is critical. During a time when "tumultuous" is a word that easily describes daily life; having the moments of peace that meditation provides is essential to healing. Even if it is difficult to quiet your mind and take the focus off of your loss, it is better to sit quietly in that effort than to engage in an intense myriad of dizzying behaviors enacted in an effort to keep busy and avoid feeling the pain.

One can easily see how meditation would benefit a person who is grieving or experiencing intense emotional pain. Emotional stress takes a huge toll on the physical body and ravages many of its natural defenses. Meditation helps to keep the body strong and healthy for the hard work of grieving. It also offers the opportunity to visualize the positive outcome you desire. It is a proven fact that the brain doesn't know the difference between what is visualized and what is real. Therefore, to visualize yourself happy, healed and whole again, on a daily basis, is a powerful way to enhance the healing process and get you to that end goal more quickly.

Take a moment and write what you realistically feel you can and will do about establishing a daily meditation practice. Writing has been shown in research studies to greatly enhance the chances of success. It makes something concrete and solidifies the commitment.

Perhaps you can only do 5 minutes upon waking or going to sleep. Perhaps you can commit to a certain guided meditation tape. Whatever you choose, make sure that it is doable in your reality. Don't set yourself up for pressure or failure. A five minute meditation consistently practiced, is better that an hour, done sporadically, under pressure.

ACCEPTANCE – GATEWAY TO PEACE

Acceptance is one of the most important attributes that any of us can seek to attain in life. When grieving however, it is essential and yet, there is probably no other time when it is more difficult to practice acceptance, because the reality that has befallen us is incredibly painful.

All the Yogis and wise teachers throughout time have taught us the value of acceptance. It promotes peace, joy, harmonious relationships, self-love and an atmosphere of mutual respect and cooperation. I suspect that if all beings valued and practiced acceptance, there would be none of the major problems and atrocities that have plagued Man since the beginning of time.

Why is this thing called acceptance so hard? Simple, because we all have within us this other thing called Ego that always thinks its right and that its way is the only way. It requires stretching and effort to see another's perspective or to believe that everything is happening exactly as it should when what is happening feels like tragedy and pain. It isn't easy to engage fully in acceptance when what is in front of you is the unacceptable; some abhorrence, some freak of nature that you are experiencing dares to call itself your reality! This is what makes acceptance so challenging. How do you accept what you hate? Acceptance is a simple concept but it isn't an easy one.

So what is it we really need to accept when grieving?

- The reality of the loss
- The outcome of the loss
- The circumstances and events leading up to the loss

- How the loss affected and changed your life
- The feelings created by the loss
- The pain and emotions created by the loss
- The time and effort required to heal from the loss
- Your unique way of grieving the loss
- Other's opinions about how you should be thinking and feeling
- Your physical condition while grieving the loss
- The unfairness of the loss
- The insensitivity even unintentional abuse of others
- The sense of powerlessness created by the loss
- The frustration and futility of the loss
- The confusing feelings created by grief
- The emotional, perhaps physical pain created by the loss
- The feelings of isolation created by loss
- The limitations of your circumstances
- The life changes brought about by loss

There are so many more things that require acceptance but these are some of the most common ones that come up for the majority of grieving people.

How do you embrace acceptance? You ask. How do I accept the unacceptable? I don't think there is one prescribed way that works for everyone, getting there is as varied and unique as the grief journey itself. Like unconditional love, acceptance is a beautiful concept and a lofty goal but one that isn't easily mastered.

I think it requires calling on our spiritual nature to really embrace acceptance. You have to have some belief that there is a reason for everything, or a lesson to learn. Perhaps a higher purpose that we can't yet see. Maybe that all beings are working on their own evolution and doing the best they can.

Sometimes it is a belief that there is an afterlife in which we will be united with loved ones who have already transitioned, which allows us to embrace *acceptance*. Sometimes it is a knowing that a higher power controls things and trusting that everything that happens is for the highest good.

Write down the aspects of your loss that are most difficult to accept. If possible, share your writing with a trusted friend.

THANKS FOR THE MEMORIES

Memories are the cherished possessions you reflect upon after someone, something or some circumstance has been torn from you life. The enormity of loss can be terrifying. That something or someone was there, and now, they are no more. Loss is a confrontation with "never again." Our memories are often the primary connection with what was.

The tragic thing that happens in loss and grief, however, is that people avoid the memories because it becomes too painful to go to them. People feel that if they can just push the memories away long enough, they will somehow be magically healed and then be able to have them without pain.

The truth is that we need the memories in order to heal. We can't put our heads in the sand, get busy and somehow be miraculously shifted. Time doesn't heal our wounds, in spite of the mistaken belief of so many that it does.

No, we heal best when we confront the memories head on, cry our tears and then shift to remembering the wonderful, joyful events that blessed and shaped our lives. Memories, for the most part, are joyful. We tend not to remember the pain nearly as well as we remember the good times. We even have a name for it: Euphoric Recall.

This is a blessing and a curse. It is a problem when we don't remember the pain and keep recreating the same difficult scenarios over and over again in our lives. But when we are dealing with grief, the happy memories are like an armada of life preservers that float out to rescue us from the stormy seas of loss.

It is not always easy to seek and embrace the memories of what we had, what we will never have again. Looking at pictures, reading letters or doing anything else that may have us revisiting those memories can be difficult because we are actively engaging in what was. To do this is to march out courageously to confront the dragon of pain, with the hope that doing what is difficult will eventually transform and heal us. Much like a foul tasting potion that has the power to end an illness, seeking and confronting the memories, in fact, honoring them and memorializing them, can be excruciatingly painful, but also one of the most powerful ways we have to heal a broken heart.

This is no small task, but fortified with gratitude and acceptance, the healing power of this process can be absolutely transformational.

I strongly encourage you to take a deep breath and dive into doing some kind of Memory Project around the loss you have experienced. This project can take any form that appeals to you. Read the instructions on doing a Memory Project and then decide for yourself what you might like to do.

Whatever you do, once completed, be sure to share it with at least one person. Speaking out loud about the project and having those words heard by other human ears, is a crucial part of the healing. Most importantly, have fun with this project and don't worry about any emotions it brings up. Just express them and move on.

MEMORIES

Please create an embodiment of beautiful memories that you have in relation to the person, circumstance or thing that you have lost. This can be a memory book, a collage, a photo album, a shadow box, a poem, a story, a song, a scrapbook, a picture, painting or sculpture, or some other type of art endeavor that is representative of your feelings about what you have lost. It will be up to you to decide how simple or elaborate you want your creation to be.

In relationships that have been painful or troubled, some people have found it therapeutic to create the memory piece about the relationship they wish they'd had rather than the one that actually existed.

The components of your memory creation can be varied. You can use pictures, either magazine pictures that remind you of something about the person, or actual photographs. You may want to incorporate treasures given to you from the person, or mementos of special occasions. You can also include poetry, artwork, music, sculptures, letters, lines of print from magazines that say something meaningful, and really anything else that captures memories of the person you have lost.

This will be something you will share with someone special and then keep for yourself. Remember, our goal is not the creation of an award-winning piece of artwork. The most important thing is that your project be representative of both the positive and negative feelings that existed in the relationship. The main purpose is to give you another means of exploring the relationship, using a more right brain medium.

ANCHORING THE GOOD MEMORIES

Sometimes, when we are feeling sad, it is hard to remember that we ever felt good. This process will assist you in recalling and holding onto the good memories. It will help you remember times when you were content, happy, and peaceful, totally at ease or having fun.

Find a quiet place where you will be undisturbed. Let your mind wander back to a time and place when you felt good. Let it be an event that is not associated with your loss. Now, feel it, see it, smell it, taste it and hear it. Savor the great feelings you had in that moment. Be there as intensely as possible. See the details, the colors, the shapes and the textures.

As you intensify the feelings of this experience, hold onto the little finger of your left hand. Hold it tight. Take a deep breath and insert those wonderful feelings right into that little finger. Anchor them there. Release the finger and just be with those good feelings for another moment.

Then, go to another event where you had wonderful feelings and do the same thing. See, hear, feel, taste and smell the event. Experience it fully, and this time, lock it into the ring finger of the left hand. Anchor it there.

Do the same with all of the fingers on this hand. You can even do the right hand if you want to, or any other body parts where you want to anchor in your good feelings.

The next time you are feeling sad, if it is not the time or place to express it or deal with those emotions, reach for one of your fingers and you will be delighted with what happens.

You now have a treasure chest of great feelings literally "in the palm of your hand" and they are available whenever you need them. Just remember; this tool is not to take the place of grieving and authentically expressing your painful feelings. This is just a wonderful, handy little helper to get you through until a better time for you to express and process your pain.

Brow Center Balancers

The strength of this Center is critical to being able to begin to think more positive thoughts and start to contemplate living in the new normal. Intellectual information is finally able to make sense as the brain is now less fogged by emotion. The activities below will help to strengthen and sharpen this center.

- Allow yourself to recline and relax, contemplating the deep blue starry night sky.
- Visualize the color indigo blue swirling at the throat. Wear indigo blue clothing.
- Exercises and Yoga Postures that activate the brow area such as Eye Exercises, Palming, Downward Dog and the Shoulder Stand.
- Aromatherapy using Rose and Sandalwood.
- Chant "Om".
- Wear Gemstones such as Clear Quartz, Sugilite, Sapphire, Labradorite, Opals, Fluorite, Kyanite and Celestite.
- Eat deep blue foods like Purple Grapes, Blackberries, Eggplant and Purple Potatoes.
- Listen to silence or simple flute music.
- Meditation using the Brow Center Mudra. The tips of the thumbs and the middle fingers should touch. The other fingers touch at the second knuckle.
- Lightly massaging the center of the forehead.

EFT Tapping Suggestions

Again, after determining what your SUDS is on a specific issue, tap on all the points shown in the chart in Chapter Two (pg. 71) As examples of the kinds of things you would tap on in this phase, here are some statements:

1. "Even though I can't stop thinking about what happened, I deeply and completely accept myself." Then tap all the points saying, "Can't stop thinking about it."

2. "Even though I can't understand why I have to go through this, I...." Then tap all the points saying, "Can't understand why."

3. "Even though it feels so unfair that this happened to me, I...." Then tap all the points saying, "So unfair! So unfair!"

4. "Even though I just can't think positively about this, I...." Then, tapping all the points, say, "Can't be positive."

5. "Even though I feel like I can never be happy again, I...." Tapping all of the points, say "Can never be happy."

After doing several rounds, assess your SUDS and repeat the statement, or adjust it to be more specific to what you are feeling.

When you feel you have reached a 0, think of a positive condition you would like to be experiencing and tap that into all of the points in 3 rounds. Here is an example: "I am peaceful and hopeful about what the future holds," or "I am capable of knowing joy and peace in my new life."

Journaling

Journaling

Journaling

CHAPTER NINE

All You Need Is Love

"There's nothing you can know that isn't known. Nothing you can see that isn't shown. Nowhere you can be that isn't where you're meant to be. It's easy. All you need is love."

The Beatles (*All You Need is Love*)

The Energy: Lighter, Open, Empathetic, Compassionate, Grateful, Giving/Serving

The Action: Engage more actively in fun, social interaction and activities that help you adjust to your new life. Find ways of being of service to others (e.g. assisting with grief groups, helping at the hospital, working for a charity). Actively look for that which elicits gratitude.

At this point in the journey, the energy is connective, compassionate, expansive, and grateful.

It needs to be amplified and interconnected with the energy of spirituality and other people.

So how do we do this? How do we find and spend time with others who will lift us out of our doldrums and isolation. It's actually quite simple - service to others. We have to get out of ourselves and out of our homes and put our focus and energy on helping others.

The emotional pain of loss and life transitions can be isolating and insolating. We can get caught in such a trap of intense self-focus that it's almost impossible to have awareness of anything else. Emotional pain seems to be on duty 24/7. If it isn't commanding our tears, it is robbing us of our sleep and our peace of mind. But here is the dirty little secret that grief doesn't want you to know: it doesn't have this kind of power when you are with others and are open to what they offer. Self-focus, sadness and fear are deeply challenged when we are in the presence of other living beings, especially if we are in the presence of others who are positively focused or in need of our help.

There are plenty of people who need assistance with their lives. As we help them, we help ourselves. It's that simple. So volunteer at the soup kitchen, babysit your grandkids, help an old lady across the street, it doesn't matter. What does matter is that you diffuse the self-focus and self-pity and access the joy and energy of giving to someone else. When you do this, you take your vibration to a higher, lighter level. And as we have already discussed, when you do that, you access the fast track to healing.

Gratitude

"Gratitude is a precious commodity not because it is scarce, but because it is so powerful. Perfection does not bring forth gratitude. Gratitude brings forth perfection. Feeling gratitude for what you have received will attract blessings to you. This is never truer than in dealing with loss."

Gail Kent, *In Death We Do Not Part*

Feeling gratitude takes us to an energetic state that is similar to the vibration of abundance. When we are in a high energetic vibration, we are far more able to attract experiences that are of a similar vibration. One of the things that is most difficult about dealing with loss and life transition, is that we are in pain and we are experiencing painful emotions. This puts us in a low vibrational state.

The Law of Attraction tells us, "Like attracts like." Therefore, when we are at a low vibration, we can only attract experiences that are of a low vibration. I know that feels discouraging because we don't want to attract more of the painful state we are in. But take heart, even when we are in emotional states that are painful, states that are not the high energy vibration that we would desire, there is a way out: Gratitude.

Gratitude is one of the highest vibrational states there is. So, even in the midst of our anguish and tears, if we can take some time to find something in our lives to be grateful for, we shift our vibration to a higher state. This actually makes us feel happier, enhances our immune system and puts us in the position to attract something good. So be grateful for the Earth and its life-supporting beauty, be thankful for your loved ones; appreciate your home and your car and the food on your table. Be thankful for your pets, your money, your work, your special gifts, and even the loss or life transition that you are going through because it has brought you into this moment. And in this moment you are a wiser, more tolerant, more appreciative, more giving, and more vibrantly alive being.

Remember, choosing joy, being of service to others, trusting that all is well, and accepting that everything is happening for our highest good, is life enhancing and very healing.

Crown Center Energy

This energy center is our spiritual connector. It impacts our capacity to allow our spirituality to become an integral part of the physical life as well as a source of guidance. It is central to having an intimate relationship with the Divine. This is the center of knowingness, inspiration and seeing the larger purpose of our lives. It is our connection with Spirit, higher mind, faith, ethics, humanitarianism and higher consciousness. It is the center of prayer and meditation and the source of devotion, inspiration, unity, Divine understanding, idealism and selfless service.

Because this center is of such a high vibration, it can take us to higher-minded levels of thinking and behavior. That is why I feel that at this point in the journey it is so critical to find a way to be of service to others. By its very nature, so much of what we experience when we are dealing with loss and transition fosters a great deal of self-focus. We are in pain and it takes self-care and nurturing to heal. However, when we emerge into this Crown Center phase, we are ready to look out into the world and find our place there again. One of the best ways to do this is to find a person, an organization or a group that we would like to serve in some way. This kind of activity is critical in the final phase of this journey. It is the life raft that will take us back to the shores of life.

At this point we are ready to move beyond loss and into a meaningful life experience again. Finding meaning in why we went through the pain of loss becomes possible now, which can be very important. It can give us a sense of purpose and hope, as well as a much deeper understanding of why we go through pain and suffering in life. Developing some kind of spiritual practice expands and expedites this growth. I highly encourage prayer, meditation, spiritual practices, or finding a church or group you resonate with.

It is here, now, that we finally feel an end to the pain and a beginning of a new life. Through the long, dark night, we have held on, and now we can finally see the dawn of a bright, new day.

Read:

An Attitude of Gratitude (pg. 214), You Got a Friend (pg. 217) Trust is a Bitch (pg. 219)

Processes To Do:

The Magical Mystery of My Tragical History (pg. 221) The Wonderful World Walk (pg. 225), The Wonderful World List, (pg. 226), I Fall Asleep Counting My Blessings (pg. 227), Crown Center Balancers (pg. 229), EFT (pg. 230)

EFT

Journal:

About the experience you have had with loss or life transition and the gratitude that you can now access in regards to it. What kinds of service could interest you? If you begin engaging in service, write about what it is bringing to you emotionally. How are you feeling about the circumstances of your new life? Is trust something that has grown for you due to this loss, or has it become more of a challenge?

Chapter Nine Articles

AN ATTITUDE OF GRATITUDE

Michael Bernard Beckwith, author and spiritual leader, says that the vibration of gratitude is one of the highest vibrations that exists. Gratitude is the fast track way to take your vibration to a guaranteed higher level, almost instantly.

What does this mean? It means if you're feeling down: gratitude. If you have a challenging day: gratitude. If your partner leaves you: gratitude.

Okay, okay, I can already hear some of you going, "Gratitude if my partner leaves me! What? How do I get into gratitude if my heart is breaking?"

Believe me, I know that's a tough one. But what I also know is that there is a gift in every challenge, a transformation possible in every tragedy. It's just hard to see it in the midst of pain because we go into a vibrational downward spiral. But my point is that as hard as it may be, the quicker you find something to be grateful for, the quicker you start raising your vibration and feeling better.

It's crazy isn't it? But it works. Just trust me and try it.

Spend some time in gratitude, no matter what your life circumstances might be. I guarantee it will lift you into an unexpectedly high vibe place.

When I was grieving the loss of my former husband and my dog within a month of each other, I was having a difficult time accepting what had happened. One of the tools that worked best for me was changing my thoughts to something I could feel gratitude about. Even when we think it isn't so, we always have a choice as to what we think about. Constantly focusing on the loss really intensifies the emotional feelings and can make it very difficult to have a balanced state for any length of time. It also puts far more stress on your physical body. Gratitude thoughts give the physical, mental, spiritual and emotional levels a moment's respite, like an oasis in the middle of the desert, a life raft on a turbulent sea.

Even though it often seemed impossible to accomplish, I would strive to find a *gratitude thought* that felt good and I would focus on that thought instead of the myriad of painful thoughts about my loss. Often, this gratitude thought was one that had nothing to do with the loss. Just because we have experienced a difficult life change, it doesn't mean that we have to think about it all the time. In the beginning, this is a very difficult concept because we are so obsessed with thoughts of the circumstances that deluge us. But after awhile, doing this flows more easily. As I progressed with using this tool on my personal journey, I was able to find more and more areas of gratitude relating to the loss. I know, it's hard to believe. But as I practiced finding gratitude, more and more gratitude presented itself.

Once you get into a gratitude aware state, you begin seeing so many things to be grateful for in every area of your life. I would find myself being grateful for parking spaces, for my warm bed at night, and for the people who loved and nurtured me in my need. I might feel gratitude for nutritious food (especially if I didn't have to cook it), for the perfect piece of wisdom appearing magically just when I needed it, or for an empty store when I needed to make a quick run and hadn't the will or the energy to do my hair and make-up. There is so much around us all the time that we can be grateful for. I really set my focus on finding those things, because I quickly realized, that it was a fast pass out of my prison of pain.

You've Got A Friend

I believe that being of service to others is critical to moving through the pain as quickly as possible. Focusing on something other than your loss is important. It reminds us that there is more in life than our pain. This helps us keep perspective and also provides a reprieve from our suffering. When pain is huge, it is all consuming. It becomes very difficult to focus on anything else. This only leads to more energy being focused on the pain. And remember, anything that you feed energy to grows. This is the last thing we want when it comes to our pain.

However, the same phenomenon will prove true if we are focused on something positive. Service to others gives us a chance to shift our focus to something positive. And through it, we step temporarily into a much higher vibration. As I have said before, whenever we raise our energetic vibration, we have automatically improved our chances of attracting a positive outcome.

Although it is normal and necessary to engage in self-focus and self-care when we are in the midst of change and emotional pain, there comes a point when we need to turn our sights to other people and other circumstances in order to avoid getting stuck in the painful scenario of the loss.

I was so fortunate when I was going through my own heartbreak because I was, by profession, a grief-counseling specialist. This meant that when I went to work, I was being of service to others just by doing my job. I had to suspend my focus on my pain and focus on the pain of my clients. It was only through experiencing this, that I realized the critical value of turning the focus from self, to others.

Now, let me be really clear; this is not the same as the old adage, "Just keep busy," which grossly misleads people into thinking that being busy is an effective way to deal with loss. It isn't about just keeping busy; it's about what you do when you are busy. Only balanced, effective activity is beneficial. Give to others in pain, in appropriate ways and appropriate increments of time. Turning into a harried, crazy person running in ten directions trying to help everyone so you can avoid your pain, will not aid your healing. It will only exhaust you and delay productive progress. Yes, it is helpful to give service to others, but don't forget to balance it with self-care. Balanced activity is the path to healing.

Trust is a Bitch

One of the areas that is most difficult for me, and for most people I know, is the area of trust. When some sort of catastrophe has turned your world upside down, the first thing to go is your sense of trust. It is so difficult to trust that all is well, trust that everything happens for the best, or trust that there is a higher power in charge of everything when you are grieving. Trust requires giving up control, and one of the most natural things to do when your world feels out of control is to try to gain a tighter hold on any control you do have. This is why grieving people have difficulty with sleep, sex, interpersonal relationships, constipation, muscle tension, headaches, heart pain and many other such ailments. All of those functions are dependent on letting go and trusting that all will be well.

Trust is a cornerstone of living with a sense of ease, peace and joy. We have to be able to trust that there is a method to the madness of life, that the sun will come up tomorrow and that the tide will rise and fall.

So much of living happily is dependent on trust. And yet, the very shock and unpredictability of loss undermines the psychological mechanisms we must have in place in order to have a sense of trust and ease in our lives.

Working on rebuilding the trust is an important aspect of the work of mourning. One of the activities that can be helpful in this endeavor is taking a little walk down *painful memory lane* in order to obtain a fresh look at how trust has played out in your life before. When you suffer loss or change, one of the things that often happens is that you feel forgotten or forsaken by God, or whoever you envision in charge of life. You may wonder why this tragedy happened to you, or to some other innocent being. In the moment, when everything looks so bleak, it is hard to remember that other difficult things have transpired in life and somehow you lived through them and they even worked out for the best.

It can be helpful to make a list of other difficult experiences you have endured and then across from that description (or on a separate sheet of paper,) list what happened and how things worked out. This will give you a concrete, physical reminder that trust is safe and that things do work out.

The process that follows is something I call *The Magical Mystery of My Tragical History.* It will give you the experience of doing something like this. Please make every effort to do it.

Chapter Nine Processes

The Magical Mystery of My Tragical History

The directions for this process will come in two parts. Please don't rob yourself of the experience by looking at the Part 2 directions before you have completed Part 1. This can be a life changing experience if you do the process as instructed.

Part 1 Directions:

Write the story of your life from the perspective of the tragedy that has taken place. This is your chance to cry, "Poor me." With no one telling you to buck up or be strong. Start as far back as you can remember. Talk about all the hurt, the mean kids at school, your mom's issues, your dad's absence, whatever you experienced that made your life tough. Bring it into the present day with the latest terrible thing that has happened to you.

Get some lined paper and begin writing on **every other line**, without reading the directions for Part 2. Really try to get into this "Tragical History." Tap into the feelings that you felt. Don't worry about your language; get it all out. As clearly as possible, express the pain and sadness that has been bottled up for years. You have suffered tremendously and no one has really wanted to hear your story. It has been so unfair and now is your chance to express all of the emotion that you have held down for years. If you prefer, you can do this on the computer and just change the line spacing for Part 2.

Part 2 Directions:

Okay, now that you have completed the story, I invite you to do two things. First, read it to a trusted friend who understands what you are doing and that this is part of a therapeutic process. Please instruct your friend to just listen without judgment or discussion. When you are finished, your friend may only say some variation of "Wow! That must have been so painful. You really had it tough."

Before you begin, tune into how you are feeling. You're probably feeling the heavy energy created by re-visiting these painful experiences. Then again, you may feel perfectly fine. There is no right or wrong way to feel. After reading, you can take some time to process how the experience was for you. Your friend should just listen intently and empathically while you talk.

Now, go back through the story and have your friend create a list of the tragic events. For example, the part about how hard school was for you because the kids teased you becomes

1. Kids at school teased me.

Go through the whole story compiling this list.

Now comes the fun part. Get a red pen and across from every tragedy on the list, write the "Gift" that you gained as a result of the experience.

For Example:

1. The kids at school teased me

1. I developed a love of reading and independence.

When this process is completed, you might even want to re-write the whole story from the perspective of the character gains and growth opportunities that each experience provided.

Here's an example:

The kids at school were cruel. They teased me mercilessly and never wanted to hang out with me. School was lonely agony. I hated going and couldn't wait to get home every day.

Revision:

The cruel, insecure kids at school gave me the opportunity to learn inner strength and independence. I became comfortable with being alone and developed a life-long love of reading.

These "positive takes" can be written on the blank lines you left open. Or feel free to re-write the whole story on fresh paper.

Bottom Line:

Even the current loss that you are experiencing, as difficult as it may be, will contribute to the depth and beauty of the whole being that you eventually become. Every experience matters, just as every person matters. Suck all of the juice out of this moment, even if it hurts more than anything you can remember. In the words of Kahlil Gibran:

"The deeper that sorrow carves into your being, the more joy you can contain.

Is not the cup that holds your wine the very cup that was burned in the potter's oven?

When you are sorrowful look again in your heart, and you shall see that in truth you are weeping for that which has been your delight."

THE WONDERFUL WORLD WALK

This is a simple process that is a real powerhouse for changing your attitude and your emotional state. It is effective because it gets you physically moving, which is good for getting energy unstuck, and because it forces the mind to focus on something positive.

I have used it successfully many times and I find it effective every time for raising my energetic vibration to a place where I can see beyond the sadness and darkness and reach a level of hope.

Directions:

Put on your sneakers and comfortable clothing. Go somewhere that makes you feel relaxed, inspired, comfortable or energized. Simply begin walking. And as you do, say, "thank you" for every sight and thought that gives you joy. You might start with gratitude that you can drive to this place or that you are able to walk. There is so much to be grateful for, don't miss anything. The smallest flower, the freshness of the breeze, or the fragrances in the air; it's all part of a creation filled with an abundance of things to be grateful for.

THE WONDERFUL WORLD LIST

This process is much like the above one except it is a writing exercise. I find it particularly effective at bedtime, but it can be done any time of day. It is also extremely effective if the life transition you are working with involves giving up some sort of addictive behavior. Whenever obsessive thoughts or cravings come up, sit down and do this process instead of indulging in something detrimental.

Directions:

Simply get out a piece of paper and begin to list all that you are grateful for. This can be people, places, things, events, or circumstances. Let your imagination run wild as you take yourself to a higher vibration by focusing on all the wonderful aspects of your life. As much as possible, feel all the good feelings that are elicited by focusing on your blessings.

I FALL ASLEEP COUNTING MY BLESSINGS

When I was deluged by my own grief, gratitude was a process I called on many a time to help me rise up out of the dredges of despair and feel that life was still worth living. One of my favorite things to do was a process I nicknamed "I Fall Asleep Counting My Blessings." Here are the simple instructions.

1. Lie in your bed ready to fall asleep.

2. Give yourself a hug and just hold the hug. This is important because we all need to be held when we are hurting.

3. Go back to the beginning of the day and as you review, just say, "Thank You," for everything that comes into your mind that was a gift or a blessing, or even a mini-blessing that day. As you continue through this review, you are imprinting on your brain how many blessings and gratitude opportunities your life is filled with. This changes your energetic vibration and allows you to fall asleep in a more peaceful, rested way. You will sleep better and your "inner child" will feel comforted by the hug you are holding yourself in.

4. Another benefit of this process is that you will quickly find that you have a heightened awareness of opportunities for gratitude as you go through your day. Things that might have blown right past you before now imprint as a gratitude experience in the moment they are happening.

5. This means that more of your day is being spent in the high vibration of gratitude. And the Law of Attraction tells us that when in this high vibe state, we can only attract experiences and things that are a high vibrational match. Isn't that good news?

To start practicing gratitude awareness, list all of the things that happened to you today that you can be grateful for. Then, once you have your list, try falling asleep tonight counting your blessings.

Crown Center Balancers

This is the center of connection with Spirit, Higher Mind, inner guidance, inspiration, humanitarianism, faith, higher consciousness and courage. This center allows us to go within and find growth and meaning in our experiences. It fosters spirituality and concern for the well-being of others. These activities will help to strengthen and energize this center and the abilities it is resonant with.

- Spend time alone on the top of a mountain or some other high place where you can experience the magnificence and silence.

- Visualize the colors violet, gold or white swirling at the crown of the head. Wear clothing in those colors.

- Exercises and Yoga Postures that activate the top of the head like rubbing the top of the head, hanging the head, Head Stand pose, the Lotus Pose and the Tranquility Pose.

- Aromatherapy using Lavender, Frankincense, Rosewood or Lotus.

- Chant "Mmmm."

- Wear Gemstones such as Diamonds, Amethyst, Iolite, Labradorite, Moldavite, Purple Fluorite, Selenite and Sugilite.

- Fast, this center thrives on being feed with air, sunlight and love.

- Sit in silence.

- Meditation using the Crown Center Mudra. Interlace your fingers with the index fingers pointing straight up. The right thumb should be on top of the left with hands on the chest.

EFT Tapping Suggestions

Again, after determining what your SUDS is on a specific issue, tap on all the points shown in the chart in Chapter Two (pg. 71) As examples of the kinds of things you would tap on in this phase, here are some statements:

1. "Even though I can't feel a spiritual connection, I deeply and completely accept myself." Then tap all the points saying, "Can't feel a spiritual connection."

2. "Even though I find it hard to help others when I feel I have been through so much, I...." Then tap all the points saying, "Hard to help others."

3. "Even though I fear the future, I...." Then tap all the points saying, "Fear the future."

4. "Even though I still can't trust God, I...." Then tapping all the points say, "Can't trust God."

5. "Even though I don't know what to believe in, I...." Tapping all of the points, say "Don't know what to believe in."

After doing several rounds, assess your SUDS and repeat the statement, or adjust it to be more specific to what you are feeling.

When you feel you have reached a 0, think of a positive condition you would like to be experiencing and tap that into all of the points in 3 rounds. Here is an example: "I am at peace and trust that all is in its rightful order." "I know that Spirit is with me and I am loved and protected always."

Journaling

Journaling

_____

_____

_____

_____

_____

_____

_____

_____

_____

_____

_____

_____

_____

_____

_____

_____

_____

_____

_____

_____

_____

_____

_____

_____

Journaling

CHAPTER TEN

In My Life

"There are places I remember all my life though some have changed

Some forever not for better, some have gone and some remain.

All these places have their moments with lovers and friends I still can recall.

Some are dead and some are living. In my life I've loved them all."

The Beatles (*In My Life*)

During our time together we have looked at the difficult, painful feelings of loss and life transitions, and we have worked with the Seven Energy Centers that embody different phases of dealing with them. These Centers helped us to be aware of the aspects of journeying through difficult circumstances and the benefits of incorporating some healthy, daily practices into our lives in order to enhance healing and the overall quality of life.

The practices we have talked about initially targeted healing emotional pain connected with the upheaval of change. Hopefully, along the way, you have realized that they improved the quality of all aspects of your life. You may have experienced improved relationships, personal satisfaction, a greater sense of fulfillment, more love, more peace, and more joy. We began by asking, "When Will This Pain Ever End?" and hopefully we have concluded that the answer is, "When we have processed and grown through all the experiences and gifts that it has brought us."

It is my hope that you will continue to incorporate the essential lessons of each phase and energy center.

- Root Center: **Feel the Pain**
- Sacral Center: **Seek Support**
- Solar Plexus Center: **Take Care of Yourself**
- Heart Center: **Express All of Your Feelings and Practice Forgiveness**
- Throat Center: **Speak Your Truth**
- Brow Center: **Think Positive, Uplifting Thoughts, Step Boldly into the New Life and Practice Gratitude and Acceptance**
- Crown Center: **Have a Regular Spiritual Practice and Be of Service to Others**

Let's explore how we can integrate three other powerful skill areas to enhance the quality of your life even further.

BE IN THE PRESENT MOMENT

The first of these skills is to be in the present moment. Simply put, this means having your body and your mind in the same place at the same time. When we have a lot of unhealed losses, this can be very difficult to do. Your thoughts are frequently being pulled out of the moment, to the past or the future. This circumstance usually ends up creating feelings of remorse, regret, anxiety or fear.

The irony is that all of these painful emotions are being created by realities that don't even exist. The only thing that actually exists is what is going on right here, right now in the present moment. Most of us spend a great deal of time out of the moment, and yet, the only place where we really exist is now, not in the past or the future. Only in the moment can we experience joy, pleasure, gratitude, peace, acceptance, and an appreciation of beauty, love and spirituality. The loveliest of life's offerings can only be experienced right here, right now.

I believe that we initially form the habit of not being present as a defense against experiencing painful reality. However, now that we have worked with tools that have enabled us to walk through and grow from that pain, we will hopefully be more courageous about creating a life that we want to be present for. It is imperative that we make the effort to break this habit and step fully into our present lives.

With awareness and effort, we can change this pattern. The process is simple. Whenever you become aware that your thoughts have drifted away, just make a conscious effort to bring them back to the present moment. Don't chastise yourself or agonize over your inability to stay present, just come back.

At first you may feel like this process is a full time job, but that's just because you've been in the habit of being gone so much of the time. Soon, you will notice that you are present more of the time, and away less frequently. You'll become aware of the fullness and richness that comes with totally experiencing your life and you will become hooked on the new habit of actually being where you are.

One of the tools that can assist you in staying present is to slow down and really pay attention to what you are experiencing and how it feels. Even if you are washing the dishes, notice how the water feels, the texture of the sponge or cloth you are using, the slipperiness of the soap. Notice everything and you will experience it more fully as you are really with it right here, right now. Here's a bonus: try this with sex and you will notice it changes it immensely.

EXPRESS YOUR FEELINGS

The second skill area I encourage you to develop is that of expressing your feelings in the moment they occur. Hopefully our time together has improved this skill already. I know that it isn't always possible, but it is a most powerful thing to do. Sometimes, the time and place isn't appropriate, or we don't have the courage. At other times doing so would only exacerbate an already explosive situation. And sometimes, we are just too hurt to speak. None of these reasons, however, should become an excuse to ignore the responsibility we have to ourselves to eventually express those feelings.

Unexpressed feelings accumulate. And too often, the accumulation is negative. It preoccupies our thoughts and prevents us from being present in the moment to live our lives fully. If we are going to maintain good mental health and strong relationships, we must develop the practice of expressing all feelings, both joyful and painful. This keeps the emotional slate clean and ready to receive the next feeling that life brings. When this is the case, we feel fully alive and we avoid the risk of becoming numb, depressed, despondent, anxious or fearful.

The emotional life is a very important aspect of our reality. It needs to be respected and treated appropriately. When we don't express our feelings fully, life takes on a kind of drab, black and white character. Transversely, when we do acknowledge and express our feelings, life becomes a rich canvas imbued with depth, interest, texture and color. Wouldn't you rather have that as your experience?

MAINTAIN EFFECTIVE, HEALTHY BOUNDARIES

Finally, the third skill that is critical to effective living is the ability to create and maintain effective, healthy boundaries. Boundaries are the means through which you protect your physical, sexual, emotional, spiritual and intellectual realities. They are the limits you set to let others know what kind of experiences you will or will not allow. They enable you to protect yourself from hurt, which makes them a critical component of healthy relationships.

Boundaries are internal and external. The internal boundaries protect the thinking, feeling and spiritual realities, while the external boundaries protect the physical and sexual realities. Healthy boundaries aren't rigid, nor are they overly permissive. Their function is to protect and control what you expose yourself to, but they should not be so rigid that they deny you appropriate, joyful experiences.

In an ideal world, everyone would respect everyone else's boundaries and we would all possess healthy boundaries of our own. Unfortunately, reality dictates that we often have to interact with people who have no sense of boundaries and whose actions are invasive to ours. At times like these, we must be especially clear and strong about what our boundaries are. We need to be able to say, "No," or "I'm not comfortable with that." "That's not acceptable," is a clear, strong statement. "This is as much as I'm willing to do," sets clear limits and protects your experience. These kinds of statements reflect Empowered Boundaries. They are critical if your interactions with others are to serve your needs as well as theirs. Empowered Boundaries enable you to successfully co-exist with people who have caused you pain.

Much of the work you have already done on this journey has served to empower your skills in the three areas we have discussed. It has made you better able to stay in the moment, express feelings as they arise and cultivate an attitude of acceptance, gratitude, and forgiveness. All of these behaviors inevitably help us to manage, enhance and balance our energy.

Finally, maintaining healthy boundaries is an act of service to ourselves and to others. It is truly one of the most loving things we can do. When fully utilized, all of these skills work to enable you to maintain healthy relationships and live your life in a way that gives you meaning, joy, freedom and full access to the truth and beauty of your every day experience. You deserve this. Don't settle for anything less.

I can't resist one final list of miscellaneous but important suggestions. These are some of the other things that helped me get through my own pain, time and time again.

1. **Don't rush it.** Allow yourself whatever time you need to heal. There is no timeline and no two people will journey through a painful life transition in exactly the same way. Although it can be terribly uncomfortable, sit with the feelings and allow yourself to experience and grow through them. It's tempting to want to hurry up and get to a better place, but the truth is that you can't get there until you are ready. Walking through the motions of looking healed doesn't fool your wounded heart. Just resign yourself to doing the work and feeling the feelings. Then, when you reach the place of being healed, it will be authentic and you will really feel like you are coming back to life.

2. **Listen to your intuition and your heart.** Tune in to the still small voice of wisdom within you. It always knows what is best. Don't analyze it or question it. This is a time to trust your heart over your head. You are dealing with an emotional issue and you can't think your way out of what you are feeling. Trust your gut. It won't let you down. Have the courage to honor and allow what you are feeling.

3. **Journal and talk it out with safe people.** It can be very powerful and healing to express your feelings through talking and sharing them. We often find our own solutions after talking things over with someone we trust. On this note, professional help can be a wise choice. There is no shame in needing it and it can help you work through the feelings far more productively.

4. **Rely on ritual and routine.** Sometimes, when your world has been turned upside down by a sudden life transition, what you need most is ritual and routine to stabilize you and help you anchor yourself. Basic activities like getting up, lighting a candle, meditating, taking your shower, brushing your teeth and eating your breakfast can have a calming effect because they are consistent and familiar. They add a concrete, centering energy to a life that seems filled with chaos and upheaval.

5. **Let go of "Why?"** The answer to "Why?" isn't always readily apparent. It can sometimes can take months, or even years, to get a meaningful perspective as to why certain events happen in your life, and sometimes we never get the answer. If you can accept this, it will save you a lot of pain and angst. Even though it is natural to want to understand why things happen, it doesn't always matter. It is what it is, and now all that matters is how you deal with it. Give yourself a break. Don't make your healing

dependent on knowing why. There are times when acceptance is the only road to peace.

With these last tips, I have given you all of the information and tools that helped me on my own journey through life upheaval and transition. Having used them, I can now enjoy without pain, the lovely memories of Gary, my friend and former husband and Sammy my beloved four-legged angel. I hope they have been of help to you. It has been my privilege to accompany you on this journey. It took courage, discipline, determination and self-love on your part to get you to this point. I am honored to have been your guide.

It is my hope that you will continue interacting with me, and with others who will offer help and wisdom, through my online community. Information on that community will be available on my web site www.paulashaw.com. Be sure to go there and join my mailing list to be kept up to date on our latest offerings. There is information, connection, wisdom and support available for you there. I look forward to continuing our relationship.

A personal closing from Paula:

Closing

Journaling

Journaling

Journaling

About The Author

Paula Shaw, CADC, DCEP is a therapist, author and renowned speaker. Traditionally trained with degrees in Education and Communications, from Long Beach State University, Paula earned her graduate counseling credentials from Loyola Marymount University, specializing in Alcohol and Drug Counseling as well as Grief-Recovery work. In 1999, Paula fell in love with the newly emerging field of Energy Psychology because of its effectiveness in producing rapid results for individuals dealing with the difficulties of life.

A visionary and innovator, as well as one of the pioneers in the Energy Psychology field Paula became one of the founding members of the Association for Comprehensive Energy Psychology (ACEP) and today serves on its board of directors.

Paula's desire to learn even more compelled her to explore the world of the Chakras. While yoga students and yoga teachers, have been uniquely aware of the value of balancing and energizing the chakra system, Paula helped contribute to bringing awareness to the masses with the completion of the first edition of *Chakras: The Magnificent Seven,* in 2002. She now has completed her second book, **When Will This Pain Ever End?** which is focused on giving people effective information, tools and processes to help them deal with the debilitating pain of grief.

PAULA SHAW

In her 24 years of experience Paula has become passionately committed to empowering clients to help themselves transform their pain into possibility. To that end, she gives them what she calls "tools to go," which are proven, cutting edge processes that can be easily learned and implemented anytime, anywhere. Paula is trained in the most effective modalities of the Energy Psychology compendium and is also a Reiki master.

In addition to her counseling, Paula lectures, writes and teaches a variety of workshops within her fields of expertise, and has been a featured speaker at several ACEP conferences over the years.

A perfect blend of talent, gifts and tools, Paula uses both head and heart to help clients transform their pain and return to productive lives as rapidly as possible because as she says: "No one has 20 years to spend on the couch anymore."

Call **(858) 480-9234** or email: **PaulaShawCounseling@gmail.com**

Visit, **PaulaShaw.com** to learn more.   YouTube.com/user/PaulaShawCounseling

Made in the USA
San Bernardino, CA
16 June 2015